The Stress Club

The Stress Club

Tami West, PhD

Morning Sky Press
Irvine, California

To purchase additional copies of *The Stress Club*, send an email to info@tamiwest.com with your contact information and the number of books you would like to buy.

Front cover art by Nicole Holle
Interior graphic designs by Tyler Holle
Jacket design by LACreative
Page layout by Win-Win Words, LLC

The Stress Club is a Morning Sky Press publication.
ISBN: 978-0-692-80294-6

Printed in the United States of America

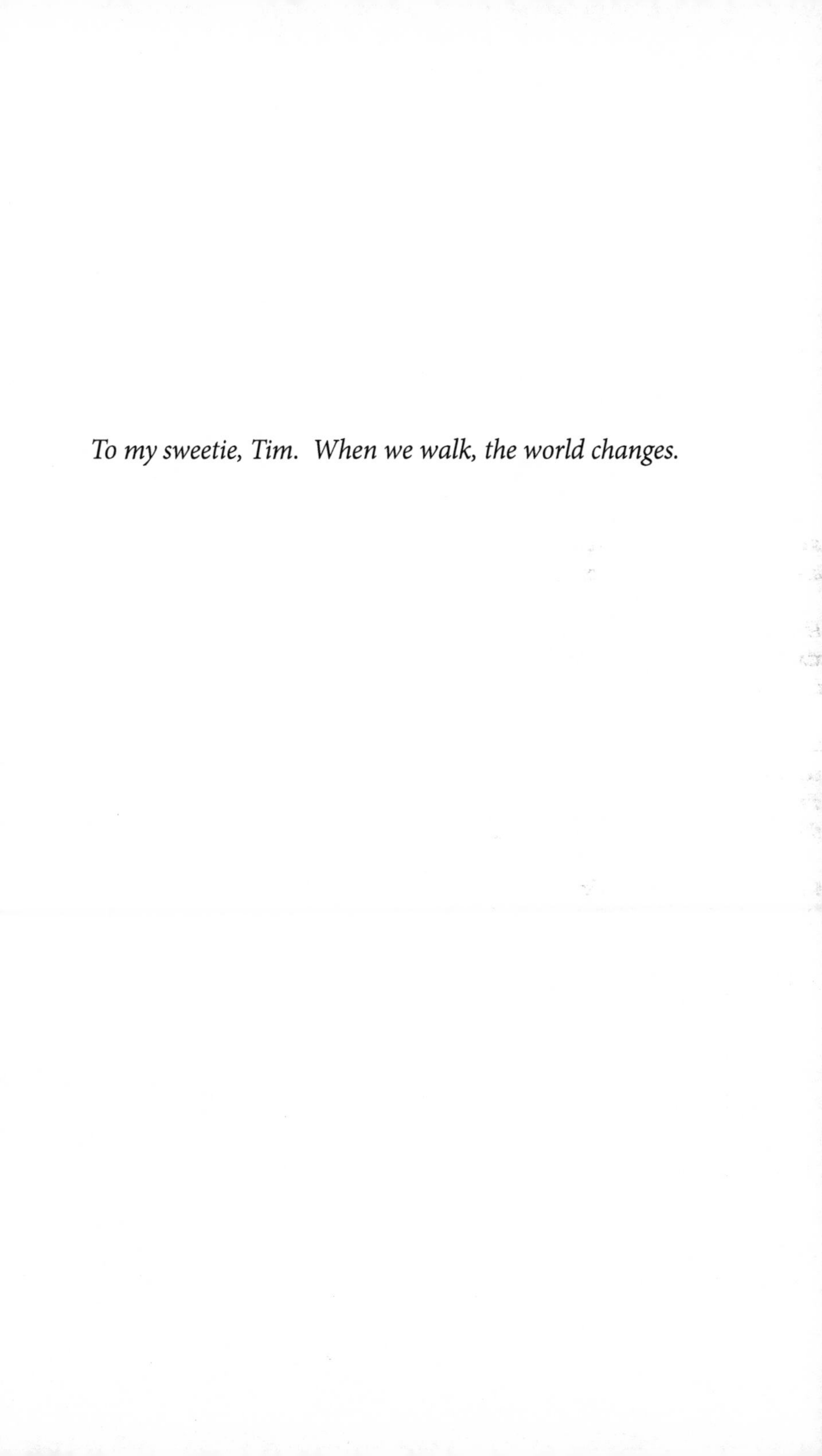

To my sweetie, Tim. When we walk, the world changes.

Contents

	Acknowledgments	ix
	Introduction	xi
	Part I: Welcome to the Club	
1	Frogs in Pots	3
2	The Fungus on the Floor	17
3	I'm NOT MAD!	33
4	My Soul Sister	43
5	Got GAS?	57
	Part II: Participating in the Club	
6	Babies, Kittens, and Puppies	77
7	Occasional Sprinkles of Fairy Dust	95
8	You Must Suffer!	107
9	That Woman in the Mirror	115
10	Push, Push, Push	133
11	Dressed to the Nines	147
	Part III: Exiting the Club	
12	Your Exit Strategy	163
13	The Night Light	199
	End Notes	209
	About the Author	211

Acknowledgments

MY NUMBER-ONE CHAMPION BEHIND THIS BOOK WAS MY HUSBAND Tim. I'm not sure whether to thank him or blame him! He first encouraged me to return to school to study something I was passionate about. Then he gave me time and space to write. He rallied me when I was tired and let me rant when I was exasperated. (OK, I guess this means I'm thanking him.)

My children, Jamie, Lindsey, and Michael, were also a constant source of support, allowing me to bounce ideas off of them, sharing my Facebook posts about stress, and encouraging me to move forward even when they were thousands of miles away.

Without the thirty women in my study, this book would only be a dream. They gave of their time, their stories, their tears, their pain, and their triumphs, and I am forever grateful to each of them.

As I reflect on the time I spent with my dissertation committee members, I realize the perfect role that each woman played. My social science background was so inadequate, and they allowed me to flourish rather than flail about aimlessly. Big thanks to Dr. Nancy Wallis, Dr. Margaret Wetherell, Dr. Judy Stevens-Long, and Dr. Georgia Persons.

Angela Howell was an enormous inspiration to me as I watched her pound the pavement with her own book. She reminded me that no one is going to be as passionate about writing and promoting our books as we are.

Finally, two special people worked with me to make the physical book as beautiful and organized as it is. My editor Mike Towle with Win-Win Words, LLC also edited *Life Without the Monsters*. He always understands my scattered style, helps me to focus my words, and fills in where I flop—*every single time!* Nicole Holle took the idea behind the book and turned the cover into a visual that is spot on. Thanks to both of them!

—Tami West, PhD

Introduction

WE NEED A REVOLUTION! NOT ONE OF BURNING BRAS OR PICKETING IN the streets (although you can do what you feel led to do.) Think of the many women who came before us in the quest to be respected and treated well. Some lived lives without respect or value. They were seen as *less than. Unimportant.* They weren't allowed to vote. Couldn't work. Didn't have opinions, at least not that they could voice. Then there was a revolution! Now, the women who came after could do it all! Right? They could bring home the bacon, fry it up in a pan. (If you don't get this reference, ask someone older than fifty.)

The revolutions that have occurred thus far have been revolutions of society telling us who we were, if and why we were important, and how we needed to live our lives. That's not the kind of revolution we need now. We need a revolution of thought, a revolution of personal action, a revolution of, well, an entirely new way of thinking. Instead of society telling us about stress—about who we are and how we should live—we need to decide for ourselves. But there's something that's holding us back. What is it?

It is June 4, 2016 and I'm walking my dog Roxie and speaking these words into my phone. It's seventy-five degrees outside, flowers are blooming, a gentle breeze rustles the leaves, a fountain nearby is dancing happily and glistening in the golden sunshine. I feel a sense of peace. But what if I called a friend, and said, *Hey! I slept great last night. It's such a beautiful morning. God has allowed me to live, at least for the time being, in this beautiful place, and I love my life!* How might she reply? How would you reply? Be honest.

I might have friends who'd support me and be happy for me, but that wouldn't be the usual case. I'm not saying I have stinky friends. . . . I'm just saying . . . in general. What I'd *probably* hear is:

Wow!

Must be nice!

Wish I had YOUR life!

Why? Why is this happening? Why do we do this? Why don't we just say, *Oh, I'm so happy for you!* and be sincere about it? What does it mean? And why has no one studied it? Is it just that we think this is the life we're supposed to live—stressful, busy, crazy, unhappy? Or is it something deeper—something from which we need to be saved? Yes to both. That's what it is. It's actually risky to relax and enjoy life. We've been unknowingly initiated into a destructive club. We've had blinders on, and it's time to rip them off.

Let's get something out of the way right here at the beginning: This book is not a therapy book. It's not a grief-counseling book. It's not a marriage book. It's not a trauma book. If you are going through something traumatic, something outside of the bounds of *normal* life (for lack of a better word), this book is not written for you. Although I know you can take away many bits of wisdom from these pages, I never want you to think I'm being insensitive to your pain. I just want to be clear that my study, my passion, and my words are directed toward living *daily life*—work, family, kids, parents, etc.—typical things that come up during the course of our days.

If you're dealing with something more tragic, I believe there are words in here just for you. You might also need help that is beyond these covers. If this is the case, *please* contact your medical doctor or go to https://findtreatment.samhsa.gov/. This site has a behavioral health treatment services locator that can help you wherever you are.

No matter who you are or why you're reading this book, you need me. And quite honestly, I need you as well, and I have truly needed you for the past ten years of my life. Writing this for the purpose of helping you has helped me more than you'll ever know. I am genetically wired in such a way that predisposes me to anxiety, fear, anger, worry, and sadness—all emotions so difficult to manage. I've been the platinum member of this horrible club! And I've had to work hard to get past that and live a life that has purpose, passion, and, yes . . . even happiness.

So who am I addressing in this book? Racecar and Pebbles (all the women selected their own pseudonyms) said it better than I could:

> ***Racecar:*** *The real world is carpools, work, school, PTA, dance, gymnastics class, soccer, burgers.*
>
> ***Pebbles:*** *On the run!*

Not just moms, though. I am addressing every woman who would say she is stressed. I am talking to every woman who feels there are not enough hours in the day. I want to help each woman who just wants to get some rest.

Let me throw out a few situations that might describe you:

- The word *stress* is pretty common in your conversations, especially with other women.
- You have a job where you work ten to twelve hours a day plus weekends. You're exhausted.
- You're a stay-at-home mom. You're *on call* 24/7 but no one appreciates or values what you do.
- Your parents are either too involved in your life or not involved enough.
- Traffic.
- Kids don't obey.

- Husband doesn't help.
- Mom drives you nuts.
- Fill in your situation

If all of them describe you, put down this book now and go get immediate help.

I've lived them all during different seasons of my life. But I have to tell you how writing this introduction actually provided a great example of everything I talk about in the book. I have struggled with writing this since the day my dissertation was finalized in July 2013. *How do I make this into a regular book? How do I structure it? How do I make it less academic?* Then my editor and I wrote a book proposal and decided it would be sixty thousand to eighty thousand words. So every time I sat down to write, I would do word counts. *What should I add here? Well, that chapter's too short. What if I just don't have that much to say?* And then I began wondering if I should write the book at all.

All of this would stress me out! Now, that is the last time you will ever hear me say something *stresses* me out. I only use the word here so you'll get me—so you'll connect with what I'm saying.

So here's the deal: I'm not wordy. I have something very specific to tell you that will change your life. I don't care if this book winds up being two hundred words or two hundred thousand words. I'm just going to write until there's nothing else to say and then stop writing. It'll be the Forrest Gump approach (remember when he ran and then just stopped running?) You won't just read a regurgitation of other people's ideas. You'll get real research, real stories, and real advice you've never heard before.

Be prepared, you will have to think. I don't mean we're doing calculus. What I mean is, you'll have to self-reflect in ways you've never done before. So . . . If you decide to read this book, if you choose believe it, if you really do the activities, if you practice, and if you give it time, your life will change. I promise!

So what makes this book different from the others on stress?

Take a look below at some of the many topics we frequently see when we attempt to learn about stress.

Stress is killing us.

Reasons to manage stress

We are women, so we're stressed.

We can't avoid stress.

Stressful world

Stress is normal.

Ways to manage stress

Choices—our responsibility

I'm not discounting the validity of any of these, but I know that something is not working. Something must be missing, or we wouldn't keep having book after book after book. It's like a puzzle: lots of information is available to help, but some pieces just aren't there; maybe they fell in the floor, and we have to find them. I discovered three missing pieces in the puzzle. What are they?

The first thing missing is the word *stress* itself—or the concept. Does it even exist? Yes, you read that correctly. You're thinking *What? Of course it exists!* But if we're going to have a word that infiltrates our very fiber of being in this world, we'd better have a deep understanding of what it means. If you go to the doctor and she diagnoses you with heart disease, you'll probably Google what that means and *then* read about the treatments or prevention. But we don't do that with stress. We just assume that it is what it is, without learning its meaning. So we'll do a fun history lesson. Don't worry, it won't be hard. Then we'll talk about the physical stuff that affects you—all the terrible things we read about. In essence, I'm going to lift off the blinders about the word.

The second missing piece is the concept of language. Think about how many times you've heard the premise that women talk more than men. Think of the comedy routines. Think about sitcoms with funny, stressed-out women. Think about the times you get together with your friends and talk about your stressed-out lives.

Think about the times you say you're *stressed-out.* And yet no one has ever studied these conversations—until me.

During our time together on this topic, you'll learn what language is. It sounds like it doesn't need explanation, but in the context of this book it does need explanation, just as the word *stress* does. We'll talk specifically about *women-talk*—which I absolutely love! I love that we talk and sometimes talk a lot. I love being part of a group of chatting women. I love that we often change the world when we speak.

Also included in our discussion of talk is a big one, and please don't be freaked out by the word: the field of Discursive Psychology. It's the study of what we're *doing* when we talk—that some kind of action is taking place. For example, consider this scenario I recently experienced: My twenty-six-year-old daughter just moved into an apartment, and I went shopping with her. In my opinion, she was spending too much money. She wanted blue sheets, so we went into Ross and I found two sets. I showed them each to her and said, "This one is twenty-five dollars and this one is seventeen dollars." Then I laughed! The first was actually $24.99—which I rounded *up*. The second set was actually $17.99—which I rounded *down*. Hmmm, do you get it? I was accomplishing something by doing that: trying to get her to spend less money. Language is not just insight into what we think and feel, action happens when we speak.

The third piece of the puzzle is the concept of our very identities—who we are as women. You'll see this sentence several times as you read this book: *If you believe that women experience more stress than men* (since you're reading this book, I'm assuming you do), *then you must believe there is a reason.* That brings me to the concept of identity. It's a misunderstood word, so during our time together we'll talk first about the basic stuff—hormones, etc. Then I'll teach you how your thoughts influence your identity and how that relates to stress.

Finally, we'll end our time together by formulating an exit strategy. I'm not truly helping you with this information unless I give you some guidance in how to apply it. As the subtitle says, I want you to stop participating in the club, take your power back, and start living your own life. I'll do that by teaching you how to change your approach to the word stress, how to change any language that is contributing to your lack of peace, and how to understand and embrace your many identities. This strategy will include some of the other self-care techniques you've learned before. What will be different is that your new stress paradigm will finally allow you to incorporate these practices and actually perform them. Without fear. Without guilt. Without risk. In fact, I'll prepare you for this plan during the preceding chapters. At the end of each chapter, you'll see real responses from women in my study—responses to the question of *What advice would you give to other women who are stressed-out?* I encourage you to pay close attention to the wisdom you'll gain from these thirty women who might be going through situations just like yours. We won't call it *stress* advice, but *life* advice.

My life has changed since my mental-hospital days. Years ago, I went to get a copy of my medical records from my 1995 stay at Parthenon Pavilion Psychiatric Hospital in Nashville, Tennessee. I was admitted with anxiety disorder, panic disorder, PTSD, and depression. I was what some would call a *hot mess.* I'll introduce myself more in Chapter 2, *My Stressed-out Path to the Mental Hospital.* I do this because there is a connection between this concept of stress and deeper issues such as anxiety, worry, and depression. While you are reading my story, I want you to consider your own story at the deepest level possible. I am like you, and you are like me—in so many ways.

In the summer of 2015 my husband Tim wanted to see those records—you know, check out the old me. He doesn't know the 1995 me (we met in 2001 and were married in 2003). He doesn't know anxious, terrified, angry me. He doesn't know the old *stressed-out* me, the me who couldn't handle life's daily doses of *fun* (you know, work, kids, home, money, friends). He never saw my outbursts of anger (well, at least not often).

Now don't get me wrong, I am not devoid of all fear and anxiety, and I still have the occasional temper tantrum. But I am not 1995 me anymore. After he read those medical records, he asked me such a powerful question:

So what made you decide to change?

Wow. I'd never thought about it like that before. I guess I did decide to change. But why? That mental hospital stay was one of the worst experiences of my life. I had hit bottom. And my breakdown wasn't even caused by a tragedy. All of it was due to circumstances of my daily life. I never want to live that way again. Sure life can be challenging, but I want to help you not be an unknowing member of the Stress Club. As much as possible, I'd like to keep you from the emotions spiral. The bottomless pit of doom. That's my passion. My mission on this planet.

Life advice from real women—Racecar and Pebbles:

> ***Racecar:*** *Well, my sister tells me all the time, don't worry about it, it will worry about itself. You worry too much. When we thought mom had cancer and I was worried to death and then we come to find out that it wasn't. She said, "Stop worrying about things.. You analyze things too much." So I'd tell someone don't do that. God's got it.*

> ***Pebbles:*** *I think that it really boils down to whether you have a personal relationship with Christ and you can let things go. I think that that's how you find your inner peace, how you can breathe occasionally when it does seem like everything's just all over you and you can't take it anymore? You just turn it over.*

Part I:

Welcome to the Club

1

Frogs in Pots

Erica: *I think when my girlfriends and I get together we all absolutely talk openly about the stresses of day-to-day life, and I do think it is pretty much the norm. I was trying to think when the last time I felt like I wasn't stressed-out and I don't really know when that was, but I will say my husband on the other hand (laughs), he doesn't seem to be stressed ever. And his job is, I mean, to me? From the outside looking in looks very stressful to me. But he just takes it in a different way. I feel like women almost harbor it. I mean, two weeks ago I broke out in a massive rash right here, and I'm still dealing with it.*

ERICA, THIRTY, IS MARRIED AND HAS NO CHILDREN. SHE IS A FULL-TIME teacher and one of the thirty women who agreed to be part of my 2013 dissertation study about how women talk about stress. The study involved casual conversations in groups of three: two participants and me. Erica's comments were from one of these conversations. Based on her description of her life, she seems stressed, right? In this one paragraph, Erica talks about deep, significant issues: gender, biology, the normalcy of stress, women and friendship, and health issues. Wow. Can you identify?

For the past ten years I have been pretty much consumed with the subject of women and stress. This began in 2007 when I was finishing up a week of presenting seminars in Virginia. Addressing a group of women, I said, "Tonight I'm flying home. Tomorrow I'm going to sleep in, get a massage, and read a book. It's important for me to take time for myself to manage the stressors in my life." The responses from the audience surprised me. The women seemed almost incensed, saying things like, "Wow—must be nice!" "Lucky you!" "Wish I could do that!" "That's not a very good use of your time!"

What's up with that? I thought. No way was I trying to elicit an impassioned response; I was simply making some closing remarks that I believed would leave everyone in a good frame of mind. My first thought was that they were acting like martyrs, like I wrote about in *Monsters*. I could visualize them swooning, wiping the sweat from their brows, thinking along the lines of *No one has it as bad as I do*. But then over the years I heard even *more* phrases during my seminars. Women were quick to interject during my sessions, and I often heard them chatting before and after the sessions. So I started writing these phrases down.

I can't/I have to!

Must be nice/Lucky you!

Well, at least you . . .

You have no idea/People don't understand!

Welcome to my world/Join the club!

You think you're stressed!

Then it hit me: stress held value for these women. They were feeding off of it. *That's it! They're getting self-worth from being stressed-out*. In a strange sort of way, they were turning a negative into a positive. *I'm stressed-out, and that makes me important, and now I get the satisfaction of letting Tami know in front of all these women. Hey, that feels good!*

I thought, *That's completely awful!* So I started telling women *not* to get self-worth from stress. I emphasized the importance of watching their words and not competing with each other for the top stress spot. I knew I was on to something with the power of language in keeping women tied to stress, but I couldn't find any research to back it up. *Was it as simple as getting worth from stress? Is it enough to simply tell women not to do that?* Speakers need to be good listeners, too, and the feedback I receive (or overhear) from seminar attendees helps me sharpen my messages for future presentations. After Virginia, I began asking women, one, if stress was a problem and, two, what they knew about how to manage their stress. This twofold question lit a fuse. One answer that jumped out was how stress was costing the country and killing us. As for stress management, the list included the usual suspects: diet, exercise, sleep, downtime, spirituality, hobbies, and so on. Most admitted they had poor diets, lousy sleep habits, insufficient downtime, and too little time left over for spiritual development. When I asked why they didn't take care of themselves, the majority said they didn't have time.

Time is certainly an issue, but I knew there was more to it. I began paying closer attention to television commercials, noticing how they were targeting stress among women. A TV ad featuring a Sealy Posturepedic® mattress, for example, depicts a woman *gold digger* who sleeps the day away. The announcer then says, "In the real world, we're lucky to get six hours of sleep. So let's get a better six." Wondering what was meant by *real world*, I discussed this ad with stress seminar participants. Once, I asked attendees to raise their hands if they got adequate sleep on a fairly regular basis. One young woman started to raise her hand, but quickly lowered it when she saw no other hands going up. Maybe she feared being ostracized by the group for having too much time on her hands.

So women weren't sleeping or taking care of themselves, but many of these same women were still seeking solutions, including through self-help books and seminars. Companies such as SkillPath and National Seminars Training offer hundreds of professional classes each year for stress management. They provide great information, skills training, and resources. I used to work for them and loved doing the training. There was something missing from the stress training, though. I knew in order to have a greater impact I had to figure out what that was—what was needed to make these classes more effective. So I once went *undercover* and visited a class presented by another seminar company, one for whom I hadn't worked. Their seminar was geared toward professional women who came to learn communication skills, assertiveness, time management, and managing emotions, among others. Two trainers conducted the class. During their opening, each gave a little blurb about the day. I was instantly intrigued when I heard one of them say this:

"Ladies . . . today we are going to give you an hour and a half for lunch! You can actually *chew* your food! Who in here ever gets to do that?"

Laughter erupted. Women nudged and poked each other, and all around you could hear comments such as, "Yeah right! I don't even take lunch, ever!" Seeing and hearing this, I thought, *Wow, they are bonding over this! What's up with that?* I had never noticed such camaraderie when it came to the subject of stress. I have since realized I, too, have contributed to these types of conversations. I have joked about how much stress women experience. I have laughed with friends over our crazy lives. Are we right to talk this way? Is stress such a real problem, as we hear, that it's appropriate to make it a priority in our conversations?

The statistics are certainly convincing. Each year the American Psychological Association publishes the *Stress in America* survey. Participants are questioned about their levels of stress, their perceptions of stress, and how they manage their stress. In the 2012 survey, 94 percent said they believed that stress contributes to the development of major illnesses; however, only 57 percent said they were doing enough to manage it. Respondents reported high stress levels, with their top stressors being money, work, and the economy. The report warned that our nation is "on the verge of a stress-induced public health crisis."[1] Other professional organizations sounding the alarm include the American Institute of Stress, which claims stress is "America's No. 1 Health Problem," and various online medical sites such as WebMD, MedLine Plus, and the Mayo Clinic, all of which provide a wealth of stress information. Each site lists definitions of stress, causes of stress, stress quizzes, and stress-management tools at hand. Maybe you have visited one, some, or all of these sites, and maybe even taken a quiz or sought advice. That's a good start; it's just not enough.

The alarm is further validated by research on the association between stress and health. Reported physical effects of stress on women include headaches, stomach ailments, skin problems, eating disorders, emotional disorders, sleep problems, heart disease, and cancer, according to the Department of Health and Human Services, Office on Women's Health, in 2010. The American Institute of Stress has reported that 75 to 90 percent of primary-care visits are for stress-related ailments. Although there is no agreement on its definition, stress is reported as a problem. Stress is killing us, right?

Economic costs are astronomical. The dollar value of job stress in America has been estimated at $300 billion a year in turnover, absenteeism, reduction in productivity, and medical, insurance, and legal expenses.[2] According to the Bureau of Labor Statistics (2001), the median number of days per year lost from work due to stress and anxiety was twenty-five, a considerably larger number than the median of sick days due to injury and illness not related to stress or anxiety. One study showed that healthcare expenditures for employees with high stress levels were 46 percent greater than those with lower stress levels.

A popular assumption is that women are more stressed than men, right? Well, they are according to the 2014 APA report (the most recent report at the time of this writing), which continues to support the premise that women are more stressed than men. This isn't exactly shocking news; many women juggle multiple responsibilities every day. Early on when writing this book, I posted a question on Facebook asking women to write one sentence answering the question, *What should be included in a book about stress?* One woman responded:

"All women are different . . . some can handle being a full-time, working, do-it-all mom. Other women who do not work, still have stress! . . . I work full time, take care of the house and laundry . . . no help from the men in my house. Tried tough love . . . has worked some . . . but not much . . . sometimes I just would like to run away . . ."

You likely know the feeling. Sometimes you just want to give up. Be done. Run away! If only someone would help!

For more than half a century books have been written about the stressed-out woman. In the 1963 book *The Feminine Mystique*, noted feminist Betty Friedan described "the problem that has no name, a vague undefined wish for 'something more' than washing dishes, ironing, punishing and praising children. In the women's magazines, it is solved either by dyeing one's hair blonde or by having another baby."[3] She described suburban housewives as living pointless days, downing tranquilizers like cough drops. She proposed a solution: Women can discover their true selves through meaningful work. Being a housewife was simply not enough. Friedan, among others, paved the way for women into the work world, and thus ratchet up the intensity of stress in their lives.

Elizabeth Pearle McKenna, in her 1997 book *When Work Doesn't Work Anymore*, described the life of a working mother: "The symptoms range from old-fashioned burnout to boredom, an increasing sense of injustice or just plain old depression. The rewards from work stop compensating for a feeling of emptiness, wasted time, and a decreased sense of purpose and importance."[4] Through her original research interviewing hundreds of working women, McKenna found that these women wanted to work, but they wanted more meaningful work. They wanted more time with family and friends, and less stress. McKenna suggested work, as structured, wasn't working for many women.

A decade later, Leslie Bennetts released her controversial book *The Feminine Mistake: Are We Giving Up Too Much?* Bennetts asserted the goal of her book was to "sound a warning horn to women who forgo income-producing work in favor of a domestic role predicated on economic dependency."[5] Like many before her, Bennetts's message was confusing to young mothers experiencing new levels of emotionality and responsibilities. Bennetts failed to advocate a work culture that embraces flexible scheduling and promotes meaningful work. She did not suggest a change in workplace values that include life outside the office: family, personal health, and wellness. Instead, she merely warned women of the dangers of not being present at work.

It seems we're just doomed to be unhappy and stressed no matter what the situation. But not to worry; there *is* help. Just watch television and you will see ads for products to help alleviate your stress. Read any woman's magazine and you'll likely see something like "Top 10 Stress Busters." You still have the seminar options for so-called "immediate" results! Most stress-management advice includes rest, proper diet, exercise, letting go, meditation, and more.

We *should* do these things, but we are not doing them, for whatever reason. So what's the deal? If all we need to do is relax and take care of ourselves to avoid this terrible world of stress, then we should do it, right? Maybe not. Here's why it's hard:

It's risky not to be stressed, as you'll be left out of the club.

Wait a minute. How can that be? I mean, it's risky to be stressed, isn't it? That's what we just covered in all those statistics. Our stress is making us sick. It's costing society millions. We're depressed and anxious and losing time at work. We're actually dying early, according to the alarms. So my claim is shocking, countercultural, and has never been made before. What you don't know is that you've become part of a club you never agreed to join: T*he Stress Club*. Women have become proverbial frogs, unknowingly dropped into a massive communal pot of water that's getting hotter and hotter each day. The club rules feel normal as you go about your day: being stressed and feeling a nagging sense of unhappiness. You don't notice it's getting worse. The club sucks you in and traps you. Before you know it you're in boiling water. But even if you recognize your membership, how do you get out? If you choose to take care of yourself and *not* be stressed, then you're out of the club, which is great. But all of your friends and family are still in, which is bad: Now you're alone. Maybe you're left out of conversations. Maybe other women make fun of you and say you must not have much going on in your life.

For women, the risk of not being stressed might be equal to or greater than that of being stressed.

This isn't an easy concept to grasp because it goes against the grain of what you are accustomed to hearing. Relaxation is usually thought of as a brief panacea, as a means to step aside from or even just abandon the rat race. Plop down on the bed or the sofa, prop yourself up with some pillows, turn on the TV, and eat chocolate and sip wine. Then when you are back up and about and engaged with life, do (or don't do) those things that together comprise a life that is more relaxed for you.

What I'm saying here goes against all that. Leaving the club is risky. Let's dig in to this some more.

Take a quick inventory of other issues you wish you could change. Is it to stop smoking? Lose weight? Eat better? Be better disciplined when it comes to deciding what to watch on TV? Or maybe to quit watching TV altogether? Deal with something even more serious such as alcoholism? None of these are simple; in each case, they are easier said than done, although there's nothing easy about dealing with alcoholism or any other addiction issue. For one thing, addiction issues are psychological as well as chemical. When it comes to eating, it sounds rudimentary: eat fewer calories than you burn. Still, we all realize it's much more complicated than that! A sticky web of issues is making it difficult to lose weight. I will tell you that relaxing and taking care of yourself is more convoluted than most of the stress-management advice floating around out there.

I'm here to help walk you through a new approach to *stress management* that will replace complicated with accessible, giving you a permanent escape route that will free you from debilitating stress and allow you to have your cake and eat it too (and it won't torpedo your next best eating plan).

In 2009 during an evening walk with my husband Tim, I was doing my typical gabbing away about seminars, women, and stress. Tim is such a patient listener. I remember telling him that night how frustrated I was that I couldn't find any research related to how women talk about things relative to the stress they experience. He looked at me and said, "Well, why don't you go back to school and study it yourself?" What a fantastic idea! Ha-ha. More about that later, but I will say I wasn't at all prepared for the stories of the women that over time

I would meet, my eventual findings, and, surprisingly, the transformation that would take place within me. The stories from the women in my study are what you'll see in this book. Names, of course, have been changed to protect their privacy.

It took me nearly two years to find a field that would help me study the phenomenon I was noticing. It's called Discursive Psychology—the study of conversations. None of my instructors or even my dissertation committee members (those faculty responsible for evaluating my study) knew much about this field of study, at least not in the manner I was approaching it. I would say to my instructors, "I want to study how women *talk* about stress." And they would say something like, "Oh, because women are stressed-out? You want to study stress?" "No," I would say, "I want to study how they *talk* about stress." Eventually I reached out to Dr. Margaret Wetherell in the United Kingdom. She is a key academic in this field of study and agreed to work with me.

There was so much I wanted to know. I wanted to understand the word *stress*. I wanted to understand how women talk. I wanted to understand who women are. I wanted to understand the messages about stress that come to us through media such as television commercials and women's magazines. Because I wanted to know so much, each time I would submit a proposal to my committee, they would say it was too much, that I needed to narrow my focus. So I did. As a result, what I'm about to discuss with you is much bigger than the sliver I was able to unravel in the early going.

I narrowed down my work to understanding ways women talk about stress and how it relates to our identities. Since my study was the first of its kind, it had to be fairly general in scope, not focusing on any one type of woman. For example, I didn't just pick moms or married women or working women or single women, etc. I reached out to a diverse group of women with the intent to recruit thirty women for my study. I sought connections through church, schools, and various local agencies with which I was familiar. The only criteria my study subjects had to meet was to identify themselves as stressed-out. It was *not* tough to find thirty. Here's the email I sent out soliciting women to be study subjects:

> "I am conducting a scientific study to learn about ways women discuss stress with each other. I am looking for women who feel overwhelmed and stressed. By this, I'm not referring to crises, but to the daily hassles of life. If this describes you, I would be honored for you to be a part of this study.
>
> "I will interview women in pairs about the stress in your lives. You may ask a friend to join you, or I will pair you up with another participant. The interview will last approximately one hour and will be conducted either in my home office or I am happy to come to you. I will not use your name in any publication.
>
> "To thank you for your time I would like to offer you a gift card to a local favorite restaurant, The Chocolate Covered Strawberry, and free copies of my publications about stress, anxiety, and happiness: *Life Without the Monsters*, *Balancing Your Career and Your Life*, and *Discovering Happiness in a Stressful World*.
>
> "The interviews will take place during the months of October and November 2012."

I closed the note with my contact information and an invitation to reach out to me so we could talk further.

An important point to repeat here is that neither the study nor this book addresses crisis situations, only what I call the daily hassles of life.

Here's a little info on the women who participated in my study: Only one pair was composed of women not already acquainted with one another. They wanted to come with their friends and/or coworkers. Their ages ranged from twenty-three to sixty-five. Two worked part-time, one was a stay-at-home mom, two were self-employed, one was a part-time student, and twenty-four had full-time jobs. Twenty-four of the women were married, five divorced, and one single. The majority, twenty-two, had children, and one was expecting her first child. Most of them came from the teaching profession—twenty of them. It's not that I more heavily recruited teachers, it just worked out that way, and it's interesting—teaching is obviously a challenging occupation. I can't draw conclusions about these demographics, but I hope someday someone will study groups according to specified demographic criteria.

During the interviews, I didn't ask asked rigid questions; I kept them generic. I had several questions to guide us, and the rest were pretty open. They went like this:

1. Do you experience stress?
2. What causes you stress?
3. Is it normal in today's society to be stressed-out?
4. Is it worse for women?
5. Is it important to take care of yourself? Why or why not?
6. Do you take steps to manage your stress?
7. If yes, what?
8. If no, why not?
9. Do you get enough sleep?
10. What does "the real world" mean?
11. How do you feel about the concept of "luck" in getting enough sleep or taking care of yourself?

I recorded these conversations, had them transcribed, and then dug in to try to figure out what might be going on.

A word about the extracts you'll be reading throughout this book. First, all of the participating women chose their own fake names for the study. So, no real names. Second, the extracts are mostly word for word, so overlook any weird grammar. I removed *um's* and extra words that made the passages difficult to read, but no content has been changed. I want this to be genuine. Next, because these were conversations, oftentimes we were all talking at the same time—imagine that! So, when someone interjected, you'll see that woman's comments in parentheses, like (**Tami:** Okay). Laughter is also shown in parentheses (.) Each woman's transcript was sent to her for her review and approval, and they graciously agreed to let me not only include their words in the dissertation itself, but also in this book.

These women were very giving of their time and were fully engaged in the interviews, so as you read these transcripts you might even be able to envision yourself and a couple of your girlfriends chatting just like these women were—that's really what it was. Notice the "mm-hmm's." Notice how often it's back and forth. And when you see the word (laughs), visualize them leaning on each other, nodding, nudging, and just being together as women.

The research I do is not the type that produces hard data, such as statistics. Likewise, what I present to you is not the law. Not every woman will relate to what's outlined here. We're not going to say this is the *norm* for women, but there does seem to be a pattern. So if some of what you read here doesn't apply to you, it doesn't mean that you're not normal.

Throughout this book you will hear the voices of women who, by taking part in the study, effectively agreed to help make your life better. Some things occurred during the interviews as expected because of how the study was structured. Other things happened that I hadn't anticipated, mainly related to the intensity of emotions during our conversations. Tears. Intimate details of lives and pain. Feelings of being overwhelmed and deeply taken advantage of. Stories of suicide, divorce, mental health issues, and more. These women held back nothing.

All of the women in my study said in some way that stress is the plight of women. All of them. We take things to heart. We carry the burden. We take care of our friends and families. They all said stress is just a normal part of life. I'm here to say otherwise.

These thirty women will always have a special place in my heart. Even though you won't know who they really are, know that long after they poured their hearts out to me they are now about to change your life.

I'm excited to be on this journey with you. I recently did a session on stress for a medical staff group conference. When it was over, a woman shared with me that when she saw the topic she thought, *Oh no! Not another stress management seminar!* But she concluded that what I said was something she had never heard before.

Erica set the stage for us here, her words telling us how women talk about stress, that it's normal to be stressed, that stress makes us sick, and that women are more stressed than men. Seems true, right? I'm here to change that. I am asking you to completely shift your thinking. In doing so, you will change your life. I want you out of the club—forever. It really is a big deal. It's risky. And I'll be with you every step of the way!

More life advice from real women—Dorian & Erica:

Dorian: *If I were to take a job at any place, not just this school, I would say, 'What are my expectations here? Besides being a classroom teacher, what other kinds of expectations would I . . . be involved in or be expected to be involved in?' I think that's very important, because I think a lot of times when they do hire new teachers . . . they find out 'Ooo, we have to do that, too.' I think it's important to not be afraid to ask questions as far as what professional responsibilities do I have. . . . So I think really knowing your expectations, and what are those that I can accept or are those that I don't have to accept.*

Erica: *The wisdom I would give is something that, not anything that I practice, but I think to the girls that I coach now I'm always saying, giving them things that, I would want them to know, but stand up for yourself, to not be afraid . . . to give your opinion, to not be afraid to say no, to understand, I mean, in the whole scheme of things, and this is when it's tough when you're a teacher, because this isn't just a job. . . . but at the end of the day it is a job. And so you can't let it, I guess, consume everything. But that's tough, that's a tough balance I think.*

2 The Fungus on the Floor

Tami: *My bags were packed, and it was time to go. even though the ride would be a short one, only half an hour, I wasn't looking forward to it. I knew I could change my mind, but that would not be a wise decision. This was the only way.*

The kids were excited! Any time Mommy and Daddy went away, they got to stay with Nana and Aunt Tina, and that was always fun. Jamie was seven, Lindsey five, and Michael three. They were too young to know that this was not just a typical getaway weekend trip for their parents. It was not necessary for them to know the real reason Mommy was leaving. They were simply looking forward to the movies, McDonald's, and staying up late with Nana and Aunt Tina.

The last week in August is usually hot and muggy as the last gasp of real summer. This time of year made me think of happier summers playing at the pool, going to the beach, and swinging at the park. This, however, had not been a happy summer, and now it was about over.

We put my suitcase in the car and waved goodbye. I managed a half smile and blew a kiss back at the kids. I didn't want them to worry.

The ride was torturous. I must have changed my mind about going a hundred times. First, "I'm not going. Take me home," and then, "No, I have to go."

How had I reached this point? What had happened to my life? Would I ever be normal again? Do I really even care? If this is my life, do I really even want to live? *All I wanted was to be normal.*

We finally arrived, found a spot in the parking garage, and entered the building. I couldn't believe this was actually happening. I was crying. I looked around and thought, All the people working here are normal. They will go home after their shifts. They might stop and get gas, maybe pick up dinner. They will go home to families or friends. They might watch a movie or go to the gym or to the mall. Why couldn't I do that?

We checked in, I signed my name, and it was done. I was now a patient in a mental hospital. This was real. When the nurses took my suitcase, it was like I was watching something from a movie, only I wasn't a spectator; I was in it. The nurses opened the suitcase and went through every single item my family had packed for me. They took my razor. My family had sent a ceramic vase filled with flowers. They took that, too, knowing it would have sharp edges if I broke it.

This was as real as it could possibly be: I was in a mental institution, and they are thinking I might try to kill myself! I wanted to go home! I was in my room all alone now—no family, not even a nurse.

I wasn't sure I could make it through this. The fear, the crying, the shaking—I felt like I was losing my mind. This was not fair! The world is going on without me, and I'm in here going crazy. I can't take this anymore! No one here even cares. They're ignoring me! Help me!

I was in a state of pure panic when the nurse finally asked the doctor if she could give me a tranquilizer. He agreed, and she gave me a pill that would allow me to calm down and sleep. Soon, the shaking slowed to a slight tremble. The crying was down to a whimper. Fear was turning to drowsiness.

How could I ever recover from this? Would I recover? Oh, God, what is going to happen to me? I have to sleep now.

AS I AM TECHNICALLY ONE OF THE WOMEN IN THE STUDY, I DECIDED TO open this chapter with my own words. I wrote that as the introduction to my book *Life Without the Monsters* in 2006. The most powerful sentence in that entire passage:

How had I reached this point?

As I wrote, I was past the deep dark life of anxiety I had lived for so long. I didn't know it yet, but my story was not complete at the time I wrote it. (I realize our stories are never complete, but I think you get what I mean.)

Have you ever gone into your jewelry box and found your necklaces so tangled up that you couldn't distinguish them? Then when you get them apart (*if* you can get them apart) you can see them as individual pieces, each different from all the others. One is long, another is short. One might be gold with beads; the one next to it plain silver. One you would wear only to a formal event, another you'd put on every day. The *Life Without the Monsters* intro I shoehorned in above is a passage I view much like I do those necklaces. My life story is a quilt woven from childhood traumas, self-esteem issues, endless choices, work, marriage, motherhood, and the list goes on. Those life situations were so jumbled together and twisted around each other that I couldn't tell them apart. I couldn't separate them in my head. My life looked like one big tangled web of parts, no two of them alike.

We women really are complicated creatures, aren't we? Our lives are an ongoing procession of stories, some good, some bad. There are old stories and new stories, and there are stories that had very little impact on us and stories that affected us deeply. We encounter other women and their own stories every day, and we might even be well aware of what's going on in their lives. Our closest friends and family might reveal their deepest secrets, thoughts, and feelings to us; and we might reveal ours to them. Then there are those women who keep their thoughts, feelings, stories, and emotions hidden. Maybe you're that way. Almost all of the women in my study expressed a shared belief that most women hide their real stories.

Meet Mishae, thirty-two, a divorced mechanic (yep, mechanic). Here's what she says about us as women:

No matter how blessed they look from the outside, like when you get to be close with them and you really see everything, you're like usually shocked.

That's probably true for many women, right? Every day we interact with women who seem to have it all together. Then we find out they're suffering. Maybe you go through life appearing to have it all together, but inside you feel like a pool of molten lava. In chapter 1, I mentioned the existence of a connection between living what we call a *stressed-out* life and deeper issues that many women struggle with: anxiety, worry, and depression. That's not to accuse stress of causing these issues, but they're certainly related. Many of the women in the study lumped together issues such as stress, anxiety, and depression. They used the words interchangeably. They talked about them in terms of causality with stress causing anxiety and depression but also anxiety and depression causing stress. The issues weren't always daily hassles. Mishae spoke of the near death of a friend, losing her financial stability, contemplating suicide. She tried antidepressants, but they didn't help. We'll hear more from Mishae soon.

Meet Kate, Candy, and Dalia (separate interviews). More about them later, but they all mentioned anxiety as we talked about stress:

> ***Kate:*** *I mean, that anxiety, you know, I've always suffered with anxiety and things like that so, that plays a part in my stress.*
>
> ***Candy:*** *I just think it's normal how you see so many people on medication now. For stress and anxiety, everyone seems to have (at least) a low level of anxiety. And that anxiety is coming from somewhere, and I think it's just from us being overloaded.*
>
> ***Dalia:*** *I have to take medication for fibromyalgia, which also, thank goodness, helps depression and the anxiety, but I can't say I enjoy life, everything to me feels like it's stressful. That could be part of where I am right now.*

Some of these women might have hidden their stories, but most seemed to share freely. I could hear and feel their pain, but what stood out most was the way they connected with each other as well as with me. The connection comes from our struggles. This is such a special phenomenon for women—one that both helps us and hurts us, as we'll soon see. For ten years I have been sharing my story about growing up with anxiety and my time in the mental hospital in 1995. I often open women's seminars by saying this:

> *Hi, I'm Tami West. I live south of Los Angeles, California. I have eight children and six grandchildren, and in 1995 I spent time as a patient in a mental hospital.*

If the women in the audience, in hearing this opening statement, happen to be looking down doodling or messing around on their phones, they quickly glance up, and then there's usually laughter and sometimes even applause (I'm not really sure what the applause means ☺). They are shocked. Is it the mental hospital or the kids that they identify with? Apparently, they look at me and don't see me as someone who would have a gaggle of kids and belong in a mental hospital. Often, at the end of the session, women are eager to share their stories with me. Somewhere in there I have broken the ice.

When I first started sharing this story, I would just move on in my presentation, saving the details for later. Since I'm not a particularly serious person, preferring instead to keep things light-hearted (or at least not to be the heavy in the room), I wouldn't share my heart or my pain with them. That finally caught up to me one day, when as soon as the session was over, a woman came up and lit into me. She said: "You made mental illness sound like a joke, and it is not!" To which I wanted to say, *Shut up! It's my story, and I'll tell it how I want to!* (I didn't, of course.)

Soon, I received another tongue-lashing, just like the first, same sort of deal, right after a session ended. I'm thinking, *Huh. Maybe I'm not getting the message to them that I think I am.* Being in a mental hospital was no joke, of course. So I decided I needed to tell them more about me and what I had been through. To share the painful part. To paint the complete picture of what that experience was like, from my perspective. Time to get serious.

My story is, I don't remember much about my childhood, but I do clearly remember the months, weeks, and days leading up to my hospital stay. Each of my three children was under the age of six, and I can remember lying in my bed, fearful, unable to get up and care for them. I remember not eating for days. I remember not coming out of my bedroom for days. I remember dropping the kids off with my mother and the drive to the hospital. I remember the twists and turns of the parking garage as we went up and up and up. I remember being left alone in a hospital room for what seemed like hours, although it probably was only minutes. The staff went through my suitcase and took everything sharp away—anything I might use to hurt myself. Although I thought about death, I don't think I would've tried to take my life. Who knows.

This was no joke. It was both the worst day and the best day of my life. It brought me here. It changed my life. It brought me to God. It forced me to examine the choices I was making. It forced me, even to this day, to maintain a close relationship with my body, my mind, my soul, and my identity. I need to live in a constant state of awareness of my story.

In the summer of 2007, I was on a US Airways flight, destination, well, somewhere! I usually don't read the magazine stuffed in the seat pocket, but for some reason, on this particular day, I did. While flipping through the pages, I was *immediately* drawn to an article titled "A Formula for Happiness." I was on my way to teach a managing-emotions class, so this completely intrigued me. According to Dr. Ed Diener, a professor of psychology at the University of Illinois, our happiness is dependent upon three factors: 1) genetics = 50 percent, 2) conditions of life = 8–15 percent, and 3) voluntary activities = 35–42 percent. It made such sense to me.

On that very day in that very seat I began to dissect my story, that is, I began to pull apart my proverbial necklaces so that I could see them individually. In a way, that day in that airplane seat was the beginning of everything that's coming to you in this book. I've talked about this *formula for happiness* many, many, *many* times since that day. But I should explain what it means and how to use and process this formula throughout your life. I will show you how to use it to learn more about yourself and why you deal with stress the way you do.

Diener and his colleagues work in a branch of psychology called

Positive Psychology—the specialty that studies our happiness. We'll use this concept of happiness in the broadest sense: how positive you are; how you respond to stressful situations, how quickly you bounce back after those events—things like that. I don't rely much on the percentages—it's impossible to separate what contributes to our emotional well-being into parts like individual necklaces. Our minds have to have some way to make sense of our lives, however. This formula gives you a framework within which to organize your stories.

Through this chapter I hope to encourage you to develop awareness of your stories and the web that is your life. I have and will continue to occasionally use the term *stress* as you're used to hearing it. But that will change. We're not quite ready to talk about our conversations and that word . . . yet. For now let's process our stories and how we currently react to life based on the formula's three parts.

Here's the plan: I am going to tell my story using these three concepts. As I present my life and you follow along, consider your life as well.

My Parents—Yikes!

According to Diener, 50 percent of my (or your) happiness comes from my genetics. I don't know about you, but this is terrible news for me. In the scheme of life, when I hear stories from others, I see mine as truly not *that* bad. It did, however, shape me into the woman I am.

My parents are both in their seventies now and not in great health. I know they did the best they could raising my sister and me. For that I honor, thank, and respect them. When your parents get older and require your help, it's very interesting—the process of figuring out how to do that. I had to let go of anger and resentment. I had to forgive. That's tough, and that's where a lot of prayer helps. Amen?

My parents are polar opposites on the genetic spectrum of emotions. My father has some anger issues that have given him personal and professional problems over the years. My mom, on the other hand, has been on most every antidepressant on the market. She has lived a life of despair and bitterness, and quite honestly that's much of what I remember about her. I will give you a glimpse of hope: that has changed within the past year—more about that later.

We inherit genes from our parents that determine what Diener calls our *set point*, kind of like an emotional thermostat. Maybe, genetically, your default might be closer to sad and stressed than happy and calm. Apparently, my set point was on the fearful side. This doesn't mean you can't tinker with your set point, because you can. Medication, meditation, and therapy are all ways to alter what your genes gave you. By the way, I've done them all.

Not only do you get those genes from your parents, many of you have the privilege of being raised by those same people. That takes us to the second factor: conditions of life.

Conditions of My Life—Yikes Again!

The good news? Only 8–15 percent of your happiness is born here. Do you find that hard to believe? I sure did. And those conditions begin the moment we're born. They include everything from age and health to education, income, and even the weather. My early conditions weren't the best. I've said I don't remember much about my childhood, but I remember enough. And as most of us know (from either therapy or sitcoms), everything goes back to our childhood!

Mom and Dad met in Columbus, Ohio, where I was born. My father was a country music singer and my mother a groupie. Shortly after they were married, they packed us up (I was four and my sister five) and took us to Nashville, Tennessee. Although the memories are fuzzy, I see the pictures. We look very happy. Mom had the trendy hairdo and sixties' clothing. Dad has his sequined country music suits, guitars, and microphones. We have some pictures where Mom was all dolled up and would actually sing on stage with my dad. We have happy vacation pictures and sweet Christmas photos and all the family moments you'd expect to see in the photo albums. Seemed to me like we had some fun.

We probably had what looked like an ideal life: a mother taking care of the children while the father worked and made the money. Since Mom was an only child, her parents—my maternal grandparents—moved to Nashville shortly after we did. They had a house on the lake, a beautiful yard and dock, and a ski boat. We stayed with them often, and Grandma spoiled the heck out of us. I'm pretty sure *that* was an amazing period of my life. As I remember it, and as I see the pictures, we did look like a happy little family. But as Mishae said, and as you know, things aren't always as they appear.

The memories of the not-so-happy childhood began when I was ten and started to see the arguments between Mom and Dad. It wasn't long before they sat us down and told us they were divorcing. When I got divorced, the well-being of my children was top priority. That wasn't so with my parents' divorce. My sister and I were smack-dab in the middle: we were in the middle of the fights, the middle of the manipulations, the middle of the anger—we were in the middle in every way. I remember one night when, bless her heart, Mom yanked us out of bed and threw us in the car to go find my dad and his "floozy." That was a fun night. She would tell us he didn't love any of us and didn't want to be with us—that he was never coming back, that we were all alone in the world. Just the three of us. Alone. On our own. She cried *all* the time and fell into a deep depression.

That's when the panic attacks began. I talked about this in *Life Without the Monsters*, so I'll just describe it the same way here. It's very difficult to put into words how a panic attack feels—especially as an eleven-year-old. There was a pattern. During the day, no problem. When night fell, however, I became absolutely terrified. Every night was the same—the fear, the inability to breathe, the sense of being out of control, and the feeling that death was surely on its way. I remember wanting to breathe, but being unable to. I remember being so scared and wanting it to go away so badly. I remember hating that I was going through it yet again! It happened night after night after night.

Dad eventually stopped coming around, and the three of us struggled emotionally and financially for years. Sometimes we wondered where food, phone, gas and electricity would come from. Cleanliness? Well, that's still a big trigger for me. We grew up in, well, the only word to use is filth. We had dogs that were not house-trained even though they were in the house most of the time, and the animal smells were sometimes overwhelming. I was embarrassed to have friends over, so I didn't. We even had the health department called on us when our grass grew to over two feet tall. They posted a notice in the yard for everyone to see. I don't remember exactly what it said, but most of those legal documents say something like *POSTED, you losers! Cut your grass or else we'll do it for you and send you the bill!* Well, maybe not that, but it was still humiliating, whatever it said. The neighbors came over to help, and all I wanted to do was crawl under a rock. *Why do we have to be the outcasts? The trash of the neighborhood. I just want to be normal and not be seen–could I have an invisibility cloak please.*

Another fond memory was the Septic Tank Funk of 1980. That old tank hadn't functioned properly in years. So when I'd take a shower the water would rise until it was halfway up my calves. I felt like I was taking a shower in my own dirt and that of my mom and my sister. Nasty. Till this day I almost have a panic attack if I have to take a shower when the drain is stopped up. At one point it had gotten so backed up that we had standing black water in our bathtub and most of our sinks. We would take sponge baths from the sink, and I remember fungi growing in the crack between the tub and the floor. It was awesome (sarcasm). I wasn't a biology teacher then, so I wasn't very interested in the little fungus on the floor.

I was sixteen at the time and working for a wonderful man, a dermatologist, who became like a father to me. Mom called me at work one afternoon crying that the whole tub was filled with black water, and I remember going outside the office, sitting on the front step, and crying. He came out to comfort me and came over to my house later that day, dug up the septic tank himself, and cleaned it out. Through the difficult times, it is amazing how God brings people into our lives that shape us in good ways even as the other stuff tries to stomp us down.

So you can imagine I spent most of my school years with this persistent feeling of being unsafe. Downtrodden. Embarrassed. Outcast. How did I compensate? Perfectionism. As long as I made no mistakes, people wouldn't think poorly of me. I desperately wanted to be like *normal* people in society. I wanted to have married parents. A clean house. A clean yard. Clean carpet. Since I couldn't control that, I could be perfect in other ways. Perfect grades. Perfect behavior. Anything I could control, I would.

Another childhood issue that added to this unpleasant life of mine was the bullying. My sister and I were both a tad overweight, plus we didn't fit in with the kids in our neighborhood. A recipe for being teased, right? Every day I would get on the bus and pray that there would be no name-calling that day: *Bertha Butt* was my favorite. But no matter how much I prayed, the name-calling came—every day. I recall one day walking home from the bus and there was snow on the ground. My hood was up, but I still heard the kids laughing behind me, and the next thing I knew I was being pelted in the back of the head with snowballs. Not the best time of my life.

This feels like a lot to share, but I want you to have an idea of my story and what my conditions were as I grew up. You have childhood stories as well. As children, conditions are, for the most part, forced upon us. I could not control the environment in which I was raised. I could not control the finances, the emotional darkness, the cleanliness, whether or not my parents protected me, or even how other kids treated me. As adults, however, we start making our own choices. This leads me to the most important part of this formula —voluntary activities.

Voluntary Activities (Choices)—There Is Hope!

I didn't call it a choice at the time, but I became the ultimate perfectionist to compensate for not fitting in: Perfect 4.0 in high school. Overloading myself in college with marriage, work, and classes, but still getting A's. Having children but still continuing to overachieve at school and work. My downward spiral began in the spring of 1992. My husband at the time had just gotten out of the military. We bought a house, and I became pregnant with my third child. Being the overachieving perfectionist that I was, I decided shortly thereafter to return to school to get a master's degree in education. I wanted to teach.

After taking most of the coursework at a local university, the time finally came for me to student teach. Student teaching is essentially "practice" teaching—a full-time, forty-hour-a-week commitment. (Actually, as anyone who knows teaching knows, it was a lot more than forty hours a week during the school year.) When I wrote about this in my first book, I said that it was both exciting *and* scary. I don't know why I wrote that—maybe what I meant to say was, it *should have been* exciting. But it totally wasn't. Only scary. I can't even begin to explain how terrified I was. Not only was I getting ready to student teach full time for nine weeks, while keeping my part-time job as a clerk at the local hospital, I was pregnant, had to care for my two small children, and was taking my final required class. Remember, though, this was how I operated. I could do it. I was strong! I was perfect.

Since this book isn't about the intricacies of anxiety, I'll spare you the details I covered in *Monsters*; here's the bulleted version of the sequence of events leading to my stay at the mental hospital:

- Teacher No. 1 and I met with my supervisor about two weeks into the semester. She did not like me. That did *not* sit well with my perfectionism. We had to find another school.
- Teacher No. 2 also did not like me *and*, in front of the entire class of thirty tenth-graders, told my supervisor that another university student was doing ten times better than I was. Oh, dear. Now my self-esteem was deeply damaged.
- I quit school, but finally finished it about a year later.
- When I graduated and tried to get a teaching job, twice I took a job, and twice I quit on the first day. *Major panic attacks!*
- I was unable to overcome my perceived failure.
- Hello, mental hospital.

I've told the story many times without realizing how much deeper it was. But it was like the necklaces. I lumped together everything. My responsibilities as a wife. A mother. A student. A worker.

A housekeeper. I called it stressful. I attributed my anxiety to my desire to do everything perfectly. As I mentioned earlier, my story was not complete. Many more things were going on in my tangled web. Things I didn't even realize until recently. Things I'll share with you as we continue.

If you've done the math, you probably realize genetics and conditions account for about 58 percent of why we react the way we do to the circumstances in our complex lives. That means we still have about 42 percent left, which I see as great news. Remember, we aren't using these numbers as facts, just as organizing tools. This helps us realize we aren't at the mercy of our genetics or what happens to us. We have choices, and we have power. We can choose different paths.

I love talking about this part of the formula. The Diener article cites an interesting study about the power of voluntary activities. A group of psychology students were assigned four activities: attend a lecture, perform an act of kindness, thank someone for something, and eat an ice cream cone. What happened? All of the activities lifted their spirits for the whole day except one: eating the ice cream cone. The happy feelings generated from eating the ice cream cone were short-lived; the positive activities, the things that left the students feeling connected, continued to give them a lift well after the event. They concluded we are social creatures and most absorbed in life when we are part of something bigger than ourselves.

But being absorbed in activities like family and work, things bigger than ourselves, can feel thankless, sometimes even like we're forced into doing things for others. Many of the women in my study described complex lives similar to mine. In general, they are running around all day and taking care of others constantly. Most of the time they don't have any help. These activities certainly lead to a feeling of connectedness, but not happiness, right?

You might think, *Oh, I identify with that!* Even if you aren't married or don't have kids, you might feel like your life is one big tangled mess. You run from the time you get up in the morning until the time you go to bed. You forget things. You're still working late into the night. You might think, *I AM focused on more than just myself—that's the problem!* You might always feel stressed.

That takes me back to the most powerful sentence in my opening story:

How had I reached this point?

My medical records described a woman without hope. A woman with no power and no choices. You read my introduction in which I expressed how I was filled with fear, pain, and despair. I didn't get there just because I was predisposed to emotional problems. I didn't get there just because of what happened during my childhood. And I didn't get there just because of choices I made. It was a web, a tangled one at that. And to this day I continue to pull out more parts.

I speak to women all over the world who say they are stressed. I see their pain. I hurt with them. I don't want them or you to suffer the way I did for so many years. It's not only about the anxiety, but also the plain, old unhappiness as well. I hurt for women who feel they have to do it all and do it without assistance. I hurt for women such as Kate and Dalia, who live in the web of anxiety and stress. The hope here is that we *can* make choices that lead to happier lives. I can't change your genetics. I can't alter what happens to you. But I *can* help with the choices.

I hope you've been processing your own stories during this chapter. My story continues to evolve. I should probably explain the eight children. I remarried in 2003 to a wonderful man with one biological son and four adopted children—his niece and nephews. It really was during the first few years of our marriage that I learned so much about myself and the choices I wanted (and needed) to make to be part of a happy marriage and family that would last. He has been an inspiration, and so have all the children. They've grown now, and I think I've grown with them. Life is good!

I wish I could delve into your mind right now and know what you're thinking. Here's why, and I'll end this chapter on this thought:

Today, a friend sent me a message that a preacher she follows on Facebook was doing an upcoming episode about anxiety. She said she was intrigued because she knew it was a topic so *near and dear to my heart.* Immediately I had a deep, visceral response! It took me by surprise. This is what went through my head: *I don't need to hear another piece of advice about anxiety. I've heard it all. What could he possibly say that's any different from anything else I've heard or read?* My heart rate went up. I could feel my muscles tighten up. It was just bizarre. So I had to process why this was happening to me.

What she might have meant by *near and dear to my heart* was that I was passionate about this topic because I write about it and teach about it. But shortly before receiving her message, I had had an anxiety relapse, and I shared it on Facebook. So I assumed she was trying to give me advice. Gosh, I didn't realize I was so bad at taking advice.

As much as I have healed, sometimes I feel like the woman Mishae described—one way outside, another way on the inside. My story is still not complete—now I realize it never will be. Maybe sometimes I hide and close myself off to advice, thinking I've heard it all. But I haven't heard it all. I hope if these thoughts and behaviors have been part of your life, you're now ready to open up. To focus on the choices you have. To stop believing that a stressed-out life is just the way it is in the world today.

Because. IT. IS. NOT! I promise. It's time to leave the club.

More life advice from real women:

Abilene: *Cultivate your friends and always set some time apart for yourself every single day. Whether it's to run, to walk, to hike, to be with your dog, whatever, there's got to be quiet time for yourself and . . . you've got to cultivate relationships with women, no matter. So often women throw away the female relationships for the male relationship. Because they think that's what they're supposed to do. It's the biggest mistake in the world, my daughter just discovered that. Because she sort of ignored her girlfriends and went off with this guy she's dating and she said that was what she was supposed to do? No. So she ended up realizing, she always keeps her rugby friends, they're like, you know, the rugby girls. The Ruggers, she calls them.*

***Alice:** People, especially before I was pregnant, like if I said to some of my friends that have children, . . . "I haven't slept" and "I'm tired" and, "I'm stressed at work" and people will say "Just wait till you have kids," and that kind of thing, and it's like you're not validated if your suffering is not the same.*

POOR ALICE! HOW ANNOYING IS THAT? ALICE, TWENTY-FOUR AND A SPECIAL education teacher, is married and pregnant. Most likely you've been one of the women in that scenario. Either you've said it or you've heard it: *Just wait till you have kids!* If you've said it, stop it for goodness' sake. Every stage of life is so wonderful and precious for what it is. Each stage also has its own challenges. Being single is wonderful in so many ways. Being married is wonderful in so many ways. Being a parent is wonderful in so many ways. Then there are the not-so-wonderful parts, but that's not we're focusing on in this book.

This excerpt from Alice may very well be the most powerful one from my entire study. I had heard women talk this way about stress for years. *I* talked like this, sorry to admit. I wondered why women often talked this way to one another. I'd read and read and read to try to find out about these comments, but couldn't find one bit of research. So I'd come up with my own ideas and reasons. Then I'd teach those ideas in my sessions—not as fact but as my opinion. I called them *stress competitions*. Remember earlier I mentioned the list of phrases not to say. I cautioned women not to compete with one another. I knew I was close to understanding what was going on, but not close enough. We'll spend more time later on this powerful story from Alice, but for now let's just say that I wanted to discover the deeper meaning to these conversations other than my previous assessment of martyrdom.

My husband talks me into things. Sometimes it's simple things like, *You should try that new coffee place!* Other times it's life changing. Remember, he's the one who talked me into going back to school. After my initial, *Oh, that's fantastic* response, reality set in. How in the world was I going to make this happen? I didn't want to just quit working and go to a building every day for four to five years, so my first challenge was to find a PhD program out there that would accommodate my desire to continue working. Eventually, I found Fielding Graduate University located in Santa Barbara, California. Their programs are focused on professionals already working in the fields of leadership and/or psychology. What drew me to them was their commitment to the type of student I needed to be: flexible and dedicated to changing the world, not just seeking a PhD. What sealed the deal was being able to tailor the program to my ultimate goal: digging into the deeper meaning of women's conversations about stress, and, of course . . . changing the world.

In March 2009 I walked into Fielding for new-student orientation, and *wow*. I had never felt so out of place in my entire life. First, it had been many years since I'd been in school, and it appeared many of these students had just finished their master's. Second, my background was biology, and it seemed everyone there was already working in a social science field; for instance, there were plenty of social workers and psychologists. They all seemed way smarter than me. (In fact, they all were, but who cares.) I didn't speak their lingo. I didn't understand their methods. And this was all before I had even started the program!

That's not all. I still had to figure out which field of study would allow me to research women's conversations about stress. I mentioned earlier that none of the faculty really grasped what I was trying to say. An email exchange comes to mind: My professor told me she didn't understand my topic and assumed what I *meant* to say was that my study would be about how women cope with various stress in their lives. Coping was not my interest. Conversations were. Other students didn't understand either. Even people close to me didn't seem to understand. They all thought I just wanted to study stress. They would say, *Oh yeah—I would definitely be a prime candidate to read THAT study, ha ha!* If they had a friend next to them, they might nudge one another and laugh and laugh. Funny thing is, they had no idea that this response was exactly the kind of thing I wanted to study—and then I just laughed and laughed!

As I progressed through the program, I had the "opportunity" to become quite an expert on receiving feedback. Recall my perfectionistic past. At Fielding, my papers never were scholarly enough. I didn't use the correct research terms. I didn't understand the structure of academic papers outside of the world of science. Ugh—it really stunk for a while. But it was worth it, because I finally found the field of critical discursive psychology. Doesn't it sound sweet and simple? Don't let it scare you off like it almost did me. The good news is my writing is pretty down to earth, so I think I can explain it at a functional level—in a way that will allow you to use it to change your life.

So what is critical discursive psychology (I'll also refer to this as discursive psychology or DP)? The easiest way to describe it is to start with this one powerful concept:

Who we are as women, our very identities, are in part created when we talk.

What, you may ask, does this have to do with stress? Well, let me tell you: *Stressed-out* is an actual identity—it's telling people who you are. Please don't be misled into thinking that I'm saying *you* are responsible for your being stressed. It's more complicated than that—enough so that it takes an entire book to dissect it. The idea that being stressed-out is part of our identities is a relatively new concept. Only during the late twentieth century did researchers start identifying it and looking into it. You've probably never been introduced to or thought much about the concept of creating yourself through your language. In fact, you probably think of language (if you think about it at all) as a way to express what you're thinking and/or feeling. In other words, we tend to think language is an insight into our minds and hearts. Period. But is it? Is it *really*?

Think about this scenario: You're ticked off at someone. Maybe you're mad at a spouse, child, friend, or coworker. You're brooding for a bit. He or she subsequently notices your anger and asks, *Are you mad?* And you say: (OK, say it with me—although it'll be funny if someone's around and you blurt this out!)

NO!

You've done it, right? Your arms were probably crossed and you might have rolled your eyes. Steam might be coming out of your ears. Inside you're planning a slow and painful revenge. But if language truly is an insight into your mind and heart, then you're not mad, right? Of course you're mad! Discursive psychology helps to explain a part of this—it's a model of language as action, not one of only thoughts. It's not an attempt to explain *how* you were feeling or *what* you were thinking when you said *no*.

Discursive psychologists attempt to understand what we *do* with our language rather than the thoughts behind our words. We believe that, although thoughts definitely influence our choice of words, neither scientists nor psychologists, nor anyone else can actually access those thoughts. And if there's no way to pull them out of our heads, then there's no way to study them either. As an example, have you ever heard or said, *Well, she just thinks the entire world revolves around her!?* That assumption is probably based on something that woman said, but there's no way I can know if she's thinking that—that the entire world revolves around her. I can't put a microscope or a swab in her brain. I can't videotape her thoughts. Even if I could, it wouldn't tell me anything. She's the only one who *truly* knows what she's thinking at any particular time. But what I *can* do is study what she might be accomplishing with her words.

Discursive psychologists acknowledge that we all have inner experiences, feelings, and thoughts. Of course you have thoughts behind your words, but no one has the scientific ability to study them. My study uses this framework to focus on what women are doing when we talk. What resources (such as word choices) are we drawing upon? How are we using the words? What are we accomplishing during the conversation? How are we creating our realities and ourselves while we talk? In other words, talk is seen as purposeful; something is happening when we speak. And because women have a unique way of talking that differs from men's, we'll spend some time looking at that in the next chapter.

Discursive psychology ("DP") gives us the freedom to ask questions different from those traditionally asked about stress. For example, if you go to a counselor because you're stressed, she might ask, *How do you feel when you work overtime and still have to care for your family?* That's a great question, but not what I want to know. I want to look at what you are doing when you speak about being stressed. Just as phrases such as *I am single*, *I am educated*, *I am a mother*, and *I am a professional woman are all identities*, I am stressed, likewise, is an identity. My study is the first to look at how women create this identity in conversation.

So How Does It Work?

A hypothetical: Let's say you are being introduced to the concept of good communication for the first time. To help you with this, you would need to understand the components of communication—such as verbal, nonverbal, listening, etc. Since DP is probably a new concept to you, you need to understand a few of its parts. In defining these parts, I'll use the formal terms first and then use more common terms going forward. In DP, there are three components, two of which I use to structure most of the book. These are: Interpretive Repertoires, Subject Positions, and Ideological Dilemmas. They might sound like fancy terms, but they really are simple. I'll show you.

1. Interpretative Repertoires

In a 2011 video lecture, Margaret Wetherell, one of the key researchers in the DP field as well as one of my committee members, beautifully describes the concept of Interpretative Repertoires[6]:

> *When we speak, we're joining in with a long history of ways in which people have packaged up the world and made sense of it. We're joining in with loads of other people's voices and a kind of conversation that's been going on for a long time.*

Don't you find this poetic and beautiful? I envision women's ghostlike silhouettes floating around me with word bubbles bouncing around in the air. In plainer language, when women speak with one another about stress, they are joining a conversation that has been going on for some time. Women have been talking about stress for many years. Now we have available to us words that come from voices past and present. We make sense of stress based on how others before us have interpreted it. These are the interpretive repertoires—words, phrases, and themes women have to choose from as they speak.

Repertoires change over time. Words, phrases, and themes have changed. Do we even use the word *housewife* anymore? I think now it's more common to say *stay-at-home mom*. And we don't say *secretary* anymore, but *administrative assistant*. And all these terms are changing even as we speak. Who knows what they'll be in another fifty years. Conversations about a multitude of topics—singleness, marriage, sports, politics—continue through time, but the words change—parlance evolves—as society changes. Let's refer to these repertoires as *themes* to make it a little more down to earth.

Since this book addresses being *stressed-out*, note that in my study I looked at ways that women talked with each other about stress. In so doing, I found three recurring themes; I'll bet you'll immediately perceive the first two, with the third requiring a little more explanation. They talked about stress as:

1. The plight of women
2. A reality of the real world
3. A way of social evaluation

These will be discussed in more detail in chapters 6–8, but as a preview for stress being a plight familiar to women, meet Jackie, thirty-four, a married part-time therapist and part-time stay-at-home mom. Here's what she says about women and stress:

> *I almost think that's one of the negatives of being a woman is that there's expectations, even if your husband does do child-care or housework, I think a woman still has the overarching responsibility. And so we have that task, domestic and relational and social. You know my husband's not out making Thanksgiving plans or making sure our Christmas cards are going to get sent out (laughs). So we're dealing with all that on top of work, and that's what's, I think, more challenging.*

This is no shock to you, is it? Expectations. Responsibility. Holiday plans. Domestic roles. *And* work! Since you're reading this book, you've probably talked like this before in some shape, form, or fashion. As I've mentioned, even single women talk this way about the plight of women. Even as enlightened as I've become through this study, I still occasionally find myself doing this! *Women this. Women that. Men this. Men that.*

It's crucial that we understand the word *stress*, what it means, and how we use it. And because our word choices are influenced by society, we'll need to take a look at what messages about stress are out there. In particular I'm referring to the media: commercials with stressed-out women. Sitcoms with stressed-out women. Magazine articles with stressed-out women. They're everywhere. So we'll address the word, the media, and all three of these themes in detail in subsequent chapters.

2. Subject Positions

There are many words, phrases, and themes to choose from during conversations that involve stress. They're part of society's daily lingo and we choose which ones to use when we're talking. When we choose, we take up a position, or another way to put it is we create an identity. For example, when it comes to singleness, single women might choose the identity of *Single because I want to be*, or *Single to be financially independent.* Two identities involving stress that stood out in my study are:

1. I am responsible.
2. I am like you.

At this point, this might not make much sense, so here's a quick preview as you meet Sondra and Jackie. Sondra, forty-three, is married with no children, and she works full-time with Jackie. In the conversation that follows, notice that Jackie is taking a position—in fact, she's creating herself, her identity—to be *like* Sondra. They had just watched the commercial for the Sealy Posturepedic mattress, the one mentioned in chapter 1, portraying a wealthy woman who is pampered and sleeps all day. Then I asked them if they got enough sleep. I love this example. Check it out:

Tami: *Do you feel you get enough sleep on a regular basis?*

Sondra: *Probably not.*

Jackie: *I was going to say yes. I think plus or minus, the awkward days I probably skid by with acceptable rates of sleep.*

Tami: *Okay, because if you said, "Well, I was going to say yes, but" . . .*

Jackie: *Oh, I was just reflecting because she [Sondra] said no.*

Tami: *Because then you just took a minute to think?*

Jackie: *Well, I'm thinking. Well, if Sondra is thinking no, then I surely can't be doing better than Sondra. (laughs) Eleven to six. Seven hours.*

Could you tell how Jackie wanted to be the same as Sondra? *I surely can't be doing better than Sondra!* And laughter. And what you couldn't see was their leaning on one another, touching arms. Bonding, in fact. Most of the time the women didn't directly say they wanted to be like each other, so this was an amazing glimpse.

So subject positions are the identities we create when we talk—super important. The societal messages, i.e., the media, are also important here, so you'll definitely hear more about that. We'll go into detail about all of this in chapters 9–11.

3. Ideological Dilemmas

We'll barely discuss this concept of DP, but I'll include a brief description to make your knowledge of this newfound field complete. You've just learned about word choices, and how we use our words to construct our identities. But we women are complicated, right? I'm going to loosely label this concept as a flip-flop, but not one with conscious intent. Recall the young woman from chapter 1 who started to raise her hand to the sleep question, but then lowered it when no one else joined her. You've just seen an ideological dilemma, a flip-flop. During conversation, some word choices (or actions in this case) and identities are risky and some safe. So we might create ourselves one way and then change—even in the middle of the same conversation. For this quick description, let's revisit Alice. Here's the entire extract from the earlier glimpse:

> ***Alice:*** *I think, sometimes the people are like, Oh, I'm not stressed-out, I'm like, well, you must not have a lot going on. (laughs) I know that sounds bad. I just want you to be honest about . . . People, especially before I was pregnant, like if I said to some of my friends that have children, . . . "I haven't slept" and "I'm tired" and "I'm stressed at work" and people will [say] "Just wait till you have kids" and that kind of thing and it's like you're not validated if your suffering is not the same.*

These are such powerful words that we'll revisit in chapter 8, but for now notice the shift—it's a shift almost in the same breath. On the one hand Alice seems to be evaluating people who say they're stressed but don't have a lot going on. Then she shifts and expresses how terrible it makes her feel when her friends do this to her.

I always want to point out powerful words from these brave women—keep this one in mind as we go forward. So powerful:

It's like you're not validated
if your suffering is not the same.

This is good stuff. *All the women I see on television, in magazines, and on the Internet are wacked-out, crazy stressed. So I'd better suffer just as much as they do.* Right?

Onward we go. Over the next ten chapters you will hear from these women and more. You will hear their stories and mine. You will think about yours. You will be joining, as Margaret Wetherell says, *in with loads of other women's voices and a kind of long conversation that's been going on for a long time.*

More life advice from real women—Jackie and Sondra:

Jackie: *For proper self-care to take place, you have to start with your calendar, your planner, your life, really, it's your life. Planner, or your calendar, is a . . . a reflection of your life and what you're doing in it. Then you have to build in how you will take care of your nutrition, your exercise, your sleep, your spiritual life; you have to plan in things that are priority for your health and well-being and do your best to make those happen.*

Sondra: *You know, for me it's really prayer. And you know there is a daily devotional that I try to do every day, it's called Jesus Calling. And it's very much meditation-based. And it's very much 'put your cares on me, remember me when you feel stressed-out, remember me, remember that I'm there' and that really calms me. And I know that I don't have to be in control of everything because I can't. None of us can. And so, really relying on God to take care of these things here. You know, even the little things, the little spats, the little whatever that happens, nothing's too little, nothing's too small. . . . Of course you've got to do practical things, but once I kind of put myself in that mindset, that I'm like this teeny tiny person in this big huge world. You know? I think I love to fly because of that realization. I've always had a love for flying. Because it puts things in perspective. Yeah.*

4 My Soul Sister

Mishae: *God placed good friends in my life, and that counterbalanced just being able to let it out and talk about what's going on with somebody. And a girl tends to care more about her girlfriend, you know, guys just don't have the sensitivity of wanting to know exactly what all happened and just being detail-oriented. We could tell each other details, what's going on, what happened, and try and help build each other up through it.*

MORE BEAUTIFUL WORDS; I SINCERELY LOVE WOMEN'S CONVERSATIONS! You met Mishae in chapter 2. Recall how I mentioned she had tried antidepressants without success. What *did* help her were her girlfriends. Notice above how she describes her girl talk: caring, sensitive, let it all out, details, helpful, building each other up. Beautiful. Now, it isn't always like that. But that's what it can be. That's what it should be. Because the world of girl talk is so complex, it has been studied . . . a *lot*. But, surprisingly, not for all that long.

Women's conversations were first studied in 1975, when Robin Lakoff's *Language and Woman's Place* outlined differences between men's speech and women's speech. I was born in 1964, so it's weird to think that women's conversations weren't particularly scrutinized until I was eleven. *Eleven*. How could no one have been curious enough to study our language before 1975? Oh, yes; Freud. We'll come back to this influential little man a bit later.

It's helpful for us to know where we've come from in all areas of my study, including our language. There were lots of women who paved the way for us, who helped us to understand our language as women. They had to be creative because of the lack of any real framework with which to start. When Lakoff wrote her book in '75, she actually used her own speech as well as that of her friends. In 1990, Deborah Tannen (I recommend all of her books) used her own marriage and those of her friends as her database for *You Just Don't Understand: Women and Men in Conversation.* In 1996 Jennifer Coates wrote *Women Talk* and admitted to secretly audiotaping conversations within her friendship circles. I would love to have been a fly on the wall when she told them, *Oh, by the way, I've been recording everything you've said for the past year.* Of course, she secured her friends' permissions before using their conversations in her books.

Lakoff, Tannen, and Coates had a lot of work to do. Prior to their research, women's language was often viewed as deficient to the *normal* language used by men. Men's language was described as vivid, robust, and characterized by depth of vocabulary. Ours, on the other hand, was labeled as weak words strung together with a lot of *ands* and *ums.* But here's the deal: Could it be that women at one time used language that matched their assigned *positions*—when they were restricted to simpler, more trivial roles and decisions? Over the next few pages, we'll look at some ideas on women's language: language as deficient, language as just different, and language as rapport. You'll meet some more women and read some examples. Think about the way you talk as you go through these sections.

Our Language Is Deficient

Prior to the 1970s, male-focused researchers described two areas in which women's language was seen as deficient. The first is related to the actual words we use. An example derives from my seminars for women when I talk about the differences between men and women, and I show a video of an adorable puppy barking at herself in a mirror. Most of the women in the room will *ooh* and *aah*, and they will nudge each other, laugh, and say things such as, *Oh, that is precious!* No one blinks an eye if we talk about things that are *sweet*, *cute*, *precious*, *adorable*, or *loveable*. But do we allow a man to fall apart at the sight of a puppy? Do we let him talk about how much he loves decorating with the color fuchsia? Do we cut him slack when he describes the beauty of the flowers in a nearby field? You don't need me to answer any of these, but I will. A man probably wouldn't be taken seriously if he used this kind of language. He might be labeled as effeminate. At this point I should mention that men have their struggles, too, that's for sure. But I didn't study men, so I don't have a lot to offer them.

On the opposite end of the spectrum is the use of powerful language, which is acceptable for men but not for women. *Oh, dear, the client canceled on me again* is different from *Oh, damn, the client canceled on me again*. Strong words are used for emphasis, to exert power, and to demand respect. We women have been taught since childhood not to use these strong qualifiers. Now, I'm not saying cursing *should* be used for clarification and power, but we know that it *is* used for those purposes. And we know that men who speak forcefully are viewed as powerful, but women as . . . well, you know the word: *b----*. What are the implications? What does this have to do with women being stressed?

If little girls learn their lessons well (meaning how to speak like *ladies*), you would think they'd be rewarded as grownups with unquestioned acceptance from society. Right? Because they played nice, they are good girls, correct? No. Rather, a girl who has grown up learning this sweet speech style might be blocked from having any real power in society. She'll likely be labeled as unable to speak precisely or to express herself forcefully. So, a girl is *damned if she does, damned if she doesn't*. If she refuses to talk like a *lady*, she is ridiculed and subjected to criticism as unfeminine, or, well, you know . . . a *b----*. If she does learn, she is ridiculed as unable to think clearly and incapable of taking part in a serious discussion; in some sense she is less than fully human. These two choices a woman has—to be less than a woman or less than a person—are painful. Understand that this places a great deal of pressure on women—pressure we often call *stress*. We're often caught between *No one listens to me*, and *No one likes me. If I speak up, what will people think?* This dilemma stinks!

A second area of *deficiency* is the way we arrange our words and use our voices, mainly tags and voice intonations. In the English language, a tag falls somewhere between a statement and a question. Certain tags can make you look less assertive. For example, the statement, T*he meeting went well, didn't it?* indicates a lack of confidence in your opinion, like you're soliciting validation. You're not sure, so you stick that little question on the end for someone to hear and confirm. This might allow you to avoid conflict by remaining vague.

Voice inflection is closely associated with tagging. Sometimes women will start to say something that sounds like a statement but then end it with a higher-pitched voice that sounds like a question. For example, a professor asks a student when she will have her paper ready, and she replies, *Um, probably by next Friday?* The rising voice on the word *Friday* sounds like a question and gives the appearance of needing approval in the same way tagging does.

Meet Roxy, a friend of Mishae's. These two women were so fun to interview—great friends with very different lives. Mishae, if you recall, is a single mechanic who shared with us her loss of income, her near-loss of a friend, and her struggle with anxiety. Roxy has quite the different life. She's a single mom struggling to make ends meet. Much of her story is centered on her desire to be a good mother and to provide for her son. Roxy shared stories of financial pain. She's been through a great deal of trauma with family and friends. Together, Mishae and Roxy continuously talked about how much it means to have the support of friends. Notice what Roxy does here as we talk about stress in society:

> *I think society is just a train wreck in itself, you know, morals and values are out the window and people have unrealistic expectations? In a way? I think? I mean, that's my personal opinion, but I think . . .*

She actually does a couple of things here: tagging *and* the voice inflection. Her comment on values and morals seemed to be a statement, but she ended it like a question. Then she added tags: *In a way? I think? My opinion.* Maybe she thought Mishae and I might disagree with her statement about society. To protect herself, she hedged a bit.

Again, what does this have to do with stress? This archaic way of thinking continues today: *women are still judged and often penalized for our language style, especially when compared to men's.* Let me disagree with these styles as weaknesses. Many have argued that these so-called deficits, such as tagging, questioning, and proper grammar, are actually skills associated with excellent persuasive communication. When, or if, we use tagging or higher inflection, it allows the person to whom we're speaking to express an opinion as well. It leaves the conversational door open and encourages more dialogue. I think Roxy was doing that earlier—keeping the door open. I love that. We need to teach young girls and women what language means. We can encourage them that they aren't weak or timid, that they can use conversation to keep dialogue open and to support one another. As women we have to be aware of the potential risks: being seen as timid or weak. But it's all about knowing who we are and why we do what we do. Let's start passing this information down.

Our Language Is Just Different

For years, women's language was a big ole deficiency. But things started to change. Remember my girl Deborah Tannen from earlier? She's a professor of language at Georgetown University and has popularized what is now called *the difference approach.* This means that men and women use different language because we belong to separate subcultures. So language differences are no more than cultural differences. In this view, boys and girls are essentially raised in two separate cultures, leading to language differences, not deficiencies. It's basically the *sugar and spice and everything nice* deal versus *snails, nails, and puppy dog tails.*

Tannen talked about common marital communication problems due to these differences. Women, she suggested, engage in *rapport talk,* while men engage in *report talk.* Maybe you have heard this before. Women talk for understanding, comfort, and support by matching their troubles with one another. For example, in conversation you might mention an unsupportive boss, and your friend might say, *Oh, I know what you mean!* This is often referred to as *troubles talk*, and it tends to be a rapport technique like *I get you girlfriend!*

Kay and Phoebe were delights to talk with as well. Both are married and full-time teachers. Kay is twenty-eight with children; Phoebe is twenty-four and has no children. You'll see in chapter 5 that Kay has been through a very difficult time the past few years—more than your typical day-to-day stuff. But she maintains a super-positive outlook on life; very inspiring. As we're chatting, Kay and Phoebe discover that both of their husbands are working on their homes. Watch for the rapport in their words:

> ***Phoebe:*** *So we just bought a house this summer. So he's thinking, like, he sent me a text the other day and he said, "When I get home I'm going to do this, this, this" at the house and he was sending me a grocery list at school, and I'm like, I would never have time to sit there and think about the things I wanted to do for the house. You know, he's thinking like,* House, house, house, house, *and I'm thinking,* School, school, school, school. *(laughs) So we're just in two different places right now. You know?*
>
> ***Kay:*** *We're in that same boat, girl. (**Phoebe:** Yeah.) We're renovating a house, and so it's like he's doing all that and I mean, I said last year I sold my soul to education. (**Tami:** Mm-hmm.) When you teach, you sell your soul to the school and that's sad that I say that but, I feel like I take away time from my kids. I feel guilty, because it's 11 o'clock, my husband's in the bed, I'm sitting there in the bed on the computer making lesson plans. You know, stuff like that. It just never ends, even if you're not doing something with school, you feel guilty, because you're getting behind.*

How many times have you been a part of a conversation like

this? Sometimes I hear women discuss a conversation with a friend and say something like, *She always tries to one-up me!* But research on girl talk supports the opposite—it's that we want to be the same. We want to connect. Notice how the bond was not just about the house issue, but it continued on into their jobs—teaching has sucked out their souls. In her audiobook *The Modern Scholar: He Said/She Said* (2008), Deborah Tannen tells a beautiful story supporting this rapport talk. I'll paraphrase:

Three young boys were playing baseball. One boy says, *My dad can hit a ball all the way to the end of the park!* A second said, *Well, my dad can hit the ball up into the trees!* But the third "wins" when he says, *Oh, yeah? Well, my dad can hit that ball all the way to the sky!*

Two young girls were talking and one says, *My mom wears contacts.* The second thought for a moment and then said, *My babysitter Amber wears contacts.* The first excitedly replies, *The same?!*

Powerful story. The boys are having a fun competition. The girls are having a connection. Now Tannen also points out that even though it might appear that the boys are engaged in a quarrelsome-type conversation, they really aren't. They laugh and shove each other and joke. So there is a connection there, but each still wants to win. For the girls, it might seem like a competition at first, when the second girl tries to come up with a story of wearing contacts. But then she smiles with excitement as she realizes they've got a connection. Again . . . beautiful.

Other women shared sweet stories of connection as well. Lydia was such an interesting woman to speak with. She's forty-two, a married full-time teacher/part-time student with children. Many of Lydia's frustrations with life stemmed from her passion for her job. She's highly dedicated to her profession and expects nothing less from those who work with her—nice! I found it fascinating, though, that when I asked what advice she would give another stressed-out woman, she said this:

> ***Lydia:*** *Talk to a friend. I talk to Dalia and . . . and she'll talk to me. So, things that we might not tell anyone else, and it helps just to have that.*

Wow! Lydia could have said *anything*: She seemed like a very driven woman, so she might have offered practical advice such as to take classes, practice yoga, rest, have a hobby . . . *anything*. But she said, *talk to a friend*. That's the rapport thing I'm talking about.

OK, one more example, as this one is just so telling for women. I need to preface it with an explanation of how it's typed here as opposed to how it really occurred. I deeply want to stay true to the actual way the conversations happened. Because this particular one is a long series of back and forths between all three of us, I decided to divide it up. When you read it, however, read *as fast as you can*. Think of times you've been with your girlfriends and it was just like a free for all! It was amazing and wonderful and real. Notice how often they interject to support each other. Notice how many times they laugh. Notice the comparison of their tasks. And finally, notice the last five words. It's a little long, but worth it:

> ***Jacqueline:*** *So that's the weekend. The weekend and that's when I feel bad about the house, so then I tried to, if I'm not so tired, then I try to get the house cleaned on Sunday. We've joined the church recently, and so Sunday morning we go to church and then for the rest of the day, we're just getting ready for the next week, by the time we do the groceries and . . .*
>
> ***Tami:*** *Do it again.*
>
> ***Jacqueline:*** *. . . clean up your house, like, there really is no weekend.*
>
> ***Grace:*** *No, I always need one more day. I always say that, if I could just have one more day.* ***Jacqueline:*** *One more day.*
>
> ***Grace:*** *Then I could—*
>
> ***Tami:*** *You said you need one more day?*
>
> ***Grace:*** *Yeah, because Friday I let myself off the hook, I don't do anything.*
>
> ***Jacqueline:*** *You just need one more day, that's how I always feel, too.*
>
> ***Grace:*** *Friday nights. Kind of relax and then I end up falling*

[asleep], I always try to get a latte on the way home thinking that'll keep me up a little?

Jacqueline: *Mm-hmm.*

Grace: *So I can watch a movie or something, no, it doesn't work (laughs), so I go to bed.*

Grace: *Right.*

Jacqueline: *Friday and Saturday morning.*

Grace: *And Saturday morning, that's when I try to get everything cleaned and all that kind of stuff and then by Saturday afternoon I kind of am like, OK, I'm going to rest for a little while, Sunday's church and then . . .*

Tami: *Do it again.*

Grace: *. . . Sunday afternoon I try to wrap up the laundry and it never gets totally done, you know?*

Jacqueline: *Mm-hmm. Or just clean and folded but not put away?*

Grace: *Not put away.*

Jacqueline: *Yeah.*

Grace: *On the table and I have, maybe two more loads, I'm like, Oh, I can't do this, I can't get this done.*

Jacqueline: *Yep.*

Grace: *So it's never always, all the way done . . .*

Jacqueline: *Mm-hmm.*

Grace: *. . . and so I feel like . . .*

Jacqueline: *If you just had, if you had one more day*

Grace: *But I'm rolling back into the week, so then it's just, like, you know, constant. Jacqueline: Yep.*

Tami: *And back again . . .*

Jacqueline: *She's my soul sister here. (laughs)*

Depending on how you count, I counted twenty-eight exchanges here, at least two laughs (sometimes those are hard to record), seven *mm-hmms*, *yeps*, and *rights*, and lots of nudges that you couldn't see. Of course I was part of the conversation, so I could absolutely feel the rapport. I hope you could as well. And those last five words: *She's my soul sister here!* There's actually much more to this conversation than just the rapport, and we'll talk about that in chapter 11.

Our Language Creates Rapport

Let's look deeper at the rapport research. When we look at our language this way, we see that when we talk, we are *doing* our gender. That must sound a little odd, so let me explain. Remember our discussion about discursive psychology? We learned that when we talk, we are *doing* something? Well, one of the things we're doing is friendship.

Another female researcher I love is Jennifer Coates. Her work is on the creation of gender and friendship during what she simply called *women's talk*. What makes her study different from those of Lakoff and Tannen is her scientific approach. In her book *Women Talk*, Coates analyzed more than nineteen hours of conversation involving friends, volunteers, and conversations previously recorded by other researchers. She concluded that, among other things, women's talk creates and sustains friendships and personal identities. So we actively create ourselves during each conversation. Coates found that women were surprised when she questioned what they *do* with their friends. They replied they don't *do* anything; they just talk. You've already met Mishae. I want to add a little more to her beautiful description from earlier of this *doing* of friendship:

> *I didn't have to take pills because God placed good friends in my life (**Tami:** Mm-hmm.), and that counterbalanced, just being able to let it out and talk about what's going on with somebody, and a girl tends to care more about her girlfriend. Guys just don't have the sensitivity of wanting to know exactly what all happened and (**Tami:** Right.) just being detail-oriented. We could tell each other details, what's going on, what happened, and try and help build each other up through it.*

Remember the words from earlier? *Let it out*, *care*, *sensitivity*, *details*, *help*, *build each other up*. Mishae reinforces the idea that our conversation is aimed at intimacy, connection, and collaboration. How amazing is it that she says she didn't have to take pills because of the friends in her life? That's a testament to the power of talk I love how Coates explained it when she noted, "Each time we speak, we are saying, 'This is a version of me.'"[7]

Bottom Line: Our Language Is Relational

Let's tie it all together. I mentioned that almost all of the women who volunteered for my study did so in pairs. They had histories and stories. Almost all mentioned the support they felt from the other person. They even shared their stories with me, someone they barely knew. They seemed to yearn for conversation. Lots of research even points to the biology of talking, that many of the verbal centers in a woman's brain are larger than a man's, and these conversations activate pleasure centers in the brain, releasing feel-good chemicals that promote intimacy. More on our biology in chapter 6.

It is during these conversations that we are able to evaluate our lives. Women's talk, an essential ingredient of women's friendships, accomplishes more than meets the eye; it includes conversations of belonging and similarity that allow us to behave in traditional *feminine* ways, such as caring and vulnerability, while at the same time allowing us to be different. Often these differences take the form of joking or humor, and they challenge one-dimensional images of womanhood.

Let's meet two more women as we close this chapter: Roscoe and Bessie. As with many of the women, they are coworkers and friends; both work in education. Roscoe is fifty-three and married with grown children. Bessie, forty-four, has grown children. I identified with them so much, because a good part of our conversation centered on our mothers. It wasn't necessarily bad, but it sure exemplified the *challenging* nature of mother/daughter relationships. As you read this, look for the frustrations, the support, the troubles' talk, and the overall rapport of these two women:

> ***Roscoe:*** *She's seventy-eight, she'll be seventy-nine in February. And not that she doesn't have a lot of wonderful qualities, too, but she drives me crazy.*
>
> ***Bessie:*** *Well, like with my parents, to me the problem, as much as anything, is they don't have enough going on in their life. (**Roscoe:** Yeah) Like I get the phone calls about "You're not going to believe what Fuzz Floyd put in my mailbox today." That's their mailman. I'm like, "What, Mama?" "Well, he put all this junk mail . . .And it doesn't even have my address on it," and I'm thinking,* Okay? Okay?
>
> ***Roscoe:*** *And I don't know about you, but my mom, being a southern woman, guilt is (**Bessie:** Ooh) a generational thing that is passed down. (**Bessie:** Yes. Yes.) And I know my grandmother guilted my mom. And I know Mom does that with her daughters. Now, my sister's a little bit better than I am sometimes at letting it just kind of roll off. I tend to, you know, and then do passive-aggressive stuff sometimes (laughs) or complain to my husband about it.*

Did you notice the agreements like *yes, yes*? There's bonding in the laughter. The *I don't know about you . . .* ? I wish you could see the camaraderie in their eyes and hear it in their voices. And as good as it is that we have that, it's the very reason stress has a hold on us so tightly: we bond over it! An important part of your *Exit Strategy* in chapter 12 will be to evaluate the language you use, especially when it comes to stress.

So this is the perfect time to move on. I just said we bond over stress, so we'd better decide what stress is.

More life advice from real women—Alice and Kate:

> ***Alice:*** *I feel like most of the things we worry about are probably something that's not that big of a deal in the grand scheme of things, and I know what helps me is just to kind of detach myself from the situation? And look at it like as someone from the outside and think is this really a big deal or not. And sometimes I can kind of let go of something and*

I think this is not in the grand scheme of things, this is not a big deal.

Kate: *Yeah, and that's hard to do, but that's really good advice. I mean, a lot of the stuff that I know that we worry about are things that, if you step back, and there are a few issues that are big, but a lot of it is just being able to look back and say this can wait till tomorrow, this is not the biggest deal. . . . I was with some friends over the weekend doing the Christmas parade thing and they're a great group of friends. We're going through a lot of the same things together, and it wasn't really about the advice as much as just sitting there and feeling, and just talking about it and feeling so not alone . . .*

5

SO WHAT IS STRESS?

Kate: *So that's stressful, I mean, I get up at five o'clock in the morning, leave my daughter all day and don't even know how I'm going to make ends meet . . .*

Racecar: *Car problems, your air-conditioning unit went out . . .*

Bernie: *Working in high school, you're working with teenagers, and big sources of stress for me are teenagers who don't seem to be held accountable for their behavior.*

Pebbles: *See, all that stuff is monetary, too. I think stress really does go back to that as a core. And . . . with my aging parents, that's my real concern. . . . I know that their health is what their health is and obviously I am concerned about their health and wanting them to stay healthy as long as possible (**Tami:** Mm-hmm), but it's (**Tami:** To take care of them.) . . . it's the money. (**Tami:** Mm-hmm.) Are we going to have enough money?*

Pebbles: *I think that that's it, sometimes it becomes so overwhelming that you think, so you just kind of like, fold and*

> *collapse and give up. I can't get it all done anyway, so I might as well not even try. Sometimes that does occur when it becomes so overwhelming. But I think for the most part most normal stressful days are just normal life days.*

I asked all the women about what stress means to them. Kate, Racecar, Bernie, and Pebbles talked about pretty *typical day* kinds of things. (Some of these women you haven't met yet, but you will.) They brought up jobs, money, health, parenthood, cars, and home issues. Most of these we might call daily life, but we also call them stress. And Pebbles says they can be so overwhelming that you just want to *fold and collapse.*

These comments were typical of most of the women. Remember Kay from chapter 4, who had been through something traumatic? At first, we talked some about her job as a teacher's aide. As we kept chatting, she divulged so much more:

> ***Kay:*** *Okay. Here goes the book. (laughs), I graduated with my teaching degree and we've got two children. One's in first grade and then one is five and so she'll start kindergarten next year. A couple years ago my sister-in-law, she went through domestic violence, just, she was abused by her husband for about two or three years that we knew of and on (date) he shot her . . . and he actually only had to serve about (time) in prison. He gets out on (date). (**Phoebe:** I'm sorry.) Oh, you're fine. So he went in in July and he got out with criminally negligent homicide, even though he admitted to his guilt, but because he accepted a plea deal, he was able to bide his time, so of course the stress of that, you know (**Tami:** Wow.) with my husband, that was his sister, you know, and he feels like he couldn't save her. So the stress of just living day to day, you know, of beating the depression, is a battle. Especially with two kids.*

This was so different from the daily challenges of work and kids. Here, we learn about a deeply traumatic event in her life and the life of her family. We hear about depression. We hear Phoebe console her. What you couldn't see was the pain in her eyes, nor could you hear the tenderness in Phoebe's voice. This event was not daily life.

This event wasn't something women would sit around together and say, *Oh, I know what you mean, girl!* This event involves police officers. Counselors. Doctors. This event takes years to begin to heal. It leaves other people to deal with the wreckage. As sympathetic and touched as I was by her story and her pain, something else jumped out at me:

We lump it all—Daycare and Murder under the same word: STRESS

I'm going to reference my book *Monsters* again. In it, I refer to the Holmes-Raphe Stress Inventory of 1967.

Take a few minutes to glance over the list. Feel free to rate yourself if you'd like.[8]

The Holmes-Raphe Social Readjustment Scale* is a list of life events with an assigned score from 11 to 100, with 100 considered the most stressful. The list comes from years of research but is certainly not exhaustive. The intent of the list is to predict a person's vulnerability to a stress-related illness. How much stress are you under?

THE HOLMES-RAHE SOCIAL READJUSTMENT SCALE

EVENTS	SCORE
Death of spouse	100
Divorce	73
Marital separation from mate	65
Detention in jail, other institution	63
Death of close family member	63
Major personal injury or illness	53
Marriage	50
Fired from work	47
Marital reconciliation	45
Retirement	45
Major change in health or behavior of family member	44
Pregnancy	40

Sexual difficulties	**39**
Gaining a new family member (birth, adoption, oldster moving, etc.)	**39**
Major business readjustment (merger, reorganization, bankruptcy, etc.)	**39**
Major change in financial status	**38**
Death of close friend	**37**
Change to different line of work	**36**
Major change in number of arguments with spouse	**35**
Taking out mortgage or loan for major purchase	**31**
Foreclosure on mortgage or loan	**30**
Major change in responsibilities at work	**29**
Son or daughter leaving home (marriage, college, etc.)	**29**
Trouble with in-laws	**29**
Outstanding personal achievement	**28**
Spouse beginning or ceasing work outside home	**26**
Beginning or ceasing formal schooling	**26**
Major change in living conditions	**25**
Revise personal habits (dress, manners, associations, etc.)	**24**
Trouble with boss	**23**
Major change in working hours or conditions	**20**
Change in residence	**20**
Change to new school	**20**
Major change in usual type and/or amount of recreation	**19**
Major change in church activities (much more/less than usual)	**19**
Major change in social activities (clubs, dancing, etc.)	**18**
Taking out mortgage/loan for lesser purchase (car, TV, etc.)	**17**
Major change in sleeping habits	**16**
Major change in number of family get-togethers	**15**
Major change in eating habits	**15**
Vacation	**13**
Christmas season	**12**
Minor violations of law (traffic tickets, etc.)	**11**

The point of the scale is predictive: *How much do you have going on at one time, and how likely are you to experience stress-related illness?* I'm all about self-assessment. In fact I love self-assessment!. But as a piece of the entire stress puzzle, it can be problematic. Once again, look at the variety of life situations on this list. And once again, they're all called stress. What does it mean?

An important step in disconnecting from stress is having a grasp on what the word really means. In chapter 1 I talked about how we're bombarded with statistics on stress, particularly women. Almost always the *new study* comes from self-report measures—you know, *How do you feel when . . . What causes you stress?, etc.* Remember that APA report I referenced? They don't give the questions word for word, but from the report, I think I can infer what was asked. So let me list how I think the questionnaire read. As you read the questions, I left blanks for you to answer. Then you can go to the 2015 report at the following link to see how you stack up to the women in the survey:

https://www.apa.org/news/press/releases/stress/2014/stress-report.pdf

Rate your level of stress on a scale from 1 to 10. ______

Has your stress increased in the past year? ______

What are your significant sources of stress?

____

What activities do you engage in to manage your stress?

____

Do you experience symptoms of stress and if so, what are they?

____

Does stress affect your sleep? ______

Does stress affect your eating habits? ______

If you took the Holmes Raphe Scale, what was your total? According to the Scale, less than 150 points indicates you have about a 50% chance of a major health problem within the next two years, and a score greater than 300 points increases your odds to 80%. And what about the APA questions? Turn the page to see the averages from the report:

- Average stress level from 1 to 10 (1 is little or no stress and 10 is lots of stress): 4.9.
- Regarding increased stress, 53% said their stress had remained the same, 29% said it had increased, and 18% reported a decrease.
- Significant sources of stress included money, work, the economy, family responsibilities, and personal health concerns.
- Reported stress management activities included listening to music, exercising/walking, watching television, and surfing the Internet.
- Symptoms of stress included irritability, anger, nervousness, anxiety, lack of motivation, feeling overwhelmed, and depression or sadness.
- Concerning sleep, 42% reported lying awake at night.
- 33% of respondents said that, because of stress, they ate too much or ate unhealthy foods.

How did you do on either or both? Do you have more stress, less stress, or about the same? It's weird to ask that, right? But in essence we're comparing ourselves to others going through similar situations. Is it possible that we're conditioned to always answer these questions in a similar way? Of course it's possible. Partly because we have all of these very credible people telling us that we're *going to die* from this stress thing! And each agency telling us this has its own ideas on stress, causes, quizzes, management tools, etc.

One more set of examples of the ambiguity of this word *stress*. I'm writing this paragraph in a hotel room in San Antonio on Sunday, July 10, 2016. I have a Google Alert set for the word *stress*, which means I get an email when news articles appear about stress. I just received a notification. More than three articles were listed, but look at just these three titles and how differently the word *stress* is used in each instance.

How will Murray handle the stress of being the favorite to win?

What does the word *stress* mean here?

- Does it mean the financial stress?
- Does it mean will he worry?
- Does it mean he'll be anxious?
- Does it mean he's not good enough?

This use of the word *stress* infers something potentially positive and life-changing in someone's career.

Being black in America is stressful.

The Dallas police officer shooting occurred just three days ago. Our nation is still mourning. So what does the word *stress* mean here?

- Does it mean dangerous?
- Demeaning?
- Scary?

Does it bother you that the same word is used to describe a career achievement and living the life of a historically oppressed race?

Survey highlights rising levels of stress for Scottish college staff.

What does the word mean here?

- Does it mean they're overwhelmed?
- Underpaid?
- Is it a dangerous job?
- Are their hours too long?

MANY jobs are called *stressful* today. In fact, I'll be bold and say *most* are described as stressful.

My favorite definition of the word *stress* comes from a couple of researchers, Ellis and Thompson, in 1983:

"Stress, in addition to being itself and the result of itself, is also the cause of itself."

At this point you might think I'm doing too much of the whole splitting hairs thing. I mean, you could argue—*You KNOW what they mean! Everyone knows what people mean when they say they're stressed. You're creating a big fuss over something simple.*

Au contraire! Recall the field of discursive psychology. When we speak, we are *doing* something. We are joining in with past and present voices. We are making word choices. We are experiencing various levels of risk. When we lump all of these life events under one word—*stress*—we lose power. We lose the ability to problem-solve during our situations. We become sucked into the normalcy of the word and don't realize there might be another way. We unknowingly become part of the Stress Club. Understanding this word we use daily is crucial to disconnecting from it and getting out.

So, how about a fun history lesson on stress? It'll be short, but so necessary. Think of the lesson this way: One benefit of reading books is being motivated and inspired, which I absolutely intend to do here for you. There's also a part of reading that involves becoming a better-informed person. That's why we had to take science in school. That's why we had to read classic literature. We need to keep learning throughout our entire lives. When you finish this chapter, you should invite your friends to get together and casually throw into the conversation some of your newfound information.

So here we go. What do women mean when we say we are stressed? Back in 1956, Hans Selye, a Hungarian doctor, gave us one of the earliest medical definitions of stress:

The nonspecific response of the body to any demand made upon it to adapt, whether that demand produces pain or pleasure.

With this definition, he gave us GAS (laughing permitted)—*General Adaptation Syndrome.* Basically what Selye said is that stress has long-lasting, detrimental effects on our bodies. He mentioned things like burnout, memory loss, anxiety, depression, the inability to cope, and stress-related illnesses. You might be thinking, *That describes me!* His description formed the basis for how we talk about stress today. It's also the foundation on which the Holmes-Rahe Scale and the APA study are built.

Now let's put it into people words. You've probably heard before that there's *good stress* and *bad stress.* That's really what Selye meant when he talked about pleasure versus pain. You can probably pull out dozens of examples of this pleasure and pain; sometimes they're jumbled up all together. Let's see if you can pick out the pain and pleasure in this story:

In January of this year (2016), my husband began seriously considering taking a job in Southern California—our home at the time was in Tennessee. Well, on March 7 he was gone—zippity fast! I stayed behind to coordinate renting out our home, packing, etc. I traveled and worked up until about a week before my April departure. So then I had to:

- Get a dumpster.
- Make sure everything was organized on behalf of my mother, who is in assisted living back in Tennessee.
- Sort through everything in our three-thousand-square-foot home.
- Decide what to take in the VW Beetle I'd be driving, what to sell, what to give away, and what to store.
- Arrange to sell things.
- Arrange to give things away.
- Get a storage unit.
- Hire movers.
- *Pack* our three-thousand-square-foot home.
- Clean everything, and then hire and supervise someone to do the final cleaning.
- Work with the rental-management company to get our renters moved in.
- Cut off all the utilities, cable, etc.
- Drive two thousand miles cross country alone with Roxie, my dog.

As I'm writing this list, I'm thinking, *Gosh, that really was a lot!* Pain, pain, pain! But actually it was going very well. I took it one bite at a time. I was alone; all I had to do was work on the move—no one to worry about. I kind of enjoyed going through years of kid boxes—so many memories. My kids came home individually for a bit and we got to reminisce. We got rid of tons of stuff we didn't need. It was actually a happy time. So . . . Pleasure, pleasure, pleasure. I really felt like it was all OK. I was excited about the move and our new adventure.

Until . . .

Five days before I was to depart for California, something pretty horrific happened: I awoke to a man breaking into my house—he stole my purse and my car.

The details: It was 4:30 A.M, and I was fast asleep—by myself. I awoke to the door alarm, *ding, ding, ding*. You know how groggy you can be when you get startled from a deep sleep. I went over to the alarm pad on the dresser, and it read *Dining Room Door Open*. The alarm wasn't actually on but the sensors still dinged. We have French doors in the dining room, and they didn't close properly, so my first thought was, *Oh, they blew open!* Yep, I was like one of those people in the horror movies you're yelling at—*Nooooo, don't gooooo!* But I went. I headed down the stairs and called for Roxie. As I kept walking, I heard some noises and thought maybe a wild animal had gotten into the house.

As I reached the bottom of the stairs, I saw the doors wide open and ran over to shut them. Turns out that noise I heard was the screen door creaking as the man was running out of the house. After shutting the doors, I turned around to see headlights in the driveway. In horror I watched him pull away. He was too far away for me to see his face, but my mind went crazy and I immediately called 911 while watching him drive slowly down our long driveway. He was driving *so* slow. At one point he stopped. At that point I ran upstairs and locked myself in the bathroom, convinced someone was still in the house. It took the sheriff thirty minutes to get there—thirty terror-filled minutes!

Finally the law-enforcement officer arrived—the house was clear. Because the intruder took so long to drive away from my house, and I was on the phone giving the deputies every move, they were able to chase him down. The bad news is he wrecked the car as they chased him, kicked out the window, and got away. The good news is, I got my purse back, he left his DNA behind on a cigarette, and they finally caught him four months later. Amazing.

Here's what struck me about this situation as it relates to our discussion of stress: It's not that Selye was wrong about his definition. In fact, it's a very good definition. My move from Tennessee to California was filled with both pleasure and pain. Abilene, Bernie, Erica, Mishae, Kay, and Kate all had some elements of pleasure and pain in their stories that you have read here. The problem is that we have taken *all* the demands in our lives: health, finances, jobs, family, friends, loss, tragedy, vacations, holidays, moves, graduations, parties, promotions, demotions, births, deaths, lack of sleep, headaches, business, marriages, divorces, *literally everything*—and we call it all *stress*. And then we say we're dying early because of it.

For many years after Selye's revelations, most of the available stress research was related to health. We hear it all the time, right? During our conversations, I didn't specifically ask about health and stress, but it came up—a lot.

> ***Erica:*** *I feel like women almost harbor it. I mean, two weeks ago I broke out in a massive rash right here and I'm still dealing with it. Now it's like somewhat going away, but now it's like peeling (laughs), so I have to put lotion on it.*
>
> ***Tami:*** *Do you think that was from stress?*
>
> ***Erica:*** *Oh, yeah, I get them (**Tami:** Okay.), I get stress rashes, yeah.*
>
> ***Erica:*** *I believe 100 percent in the doctor-related visits caused by stress, because I swear, every single time I get sick it's like after a couple-week period or two or three weeks where it's been more than usual. And I mean, I ended up having to get my tonsils taken out two or three years ago, once again I did it over Christmas break. I did it the Friday that we went into Christmas break, spent two weeks not being able to eat or do anything, and then came back to school knowing good and well I could not miss two weeks.*

I am certainly not arguing against a mind-body connection when it comes to illness. Cortisol is real. Heart disease, high blood pressure, headaches, and sleeplessness—they're all real. But again, as I keep saying, should we keep labeling it all with this broad term called *stress*? Is this limiting our power? Our choices?

You briefly met Erica—thirty, married, and a full-time teacher/coach—in chapter 1. Much of our conversation centered around the high level of expectations from the private school where she teaches. She described evenings of exhaustion, sometimes collapsing on her couch before 8:00 P.M. Her hours are long. Her job can be thankless, especially when it comes to the school's administrators, who she says pretend to care about the personal lives of teachers but in truth only care about keeping their jobs. Erica doesn't have children, and she has mentioned how the expectations among those folks who know her are skewed—many of them assume she has loads of free time. Her life is crazy, and she goes nonstop. Could this have caused her rash? Possibly, but what is it, exactly, about her situation that would cause that? Calling it *stress* keeps Erica from identifying the specific parts of her life that could lead to health problems.

Interestingly (well, at least *I* find it interesting), a connection between life circumstances and health problems dates back not just decades, but centuries—a whole lot of centuries, in fact. We can go as far back as 2450 BC. The ancient Egyptians used verbal ceremonies and spells to combat diseases that they believed were caused by the gods. In the fourth century, Greek physician Hippocrates linked emotions to asthma; he recommended that asthmatics guard themselves against their own anger as a means of preventing an attack. At some point someone had to ask the question if this concept of stress was more than just physical, maybe also psychological. Surely there are other women out there who have lives similar to Erica, but without a rash to show for it.

So in the 1980s the focus of health/stress research changed more to how you *think* about the demands in your life and the choices you make to adapt. Researchers who focus on thoughts (the perception approach) ask the question, *Why do people respond differently to the exact same event?* For many in the field of psychology, the simple answer to that question is perception. Another researcher, Lazarus, offered this definition of stress[9]:

Stress occurs when an individual perceives that the demands of an external situation are beyond his or her perceived ability to cope with them.

In other words, two women (or more) can have the exact same life situation, but one might call it stressful and the other might not. It's all about how we think about the situation. So here we've moved away from the effects on the body to the effects on the mind. Listen as Mishae and Abilene talk about the concept of perception:

> ***Mishae:*** *You're not supposed to look stressed all the time, you're not, you know, and I'm not saying hide it, but like as Joyce Meyer says, it's a battlefield of the mind, you know. Like, you have to control it in your mind. It can be horrible or it can be you can get through this and you can build up and the more you control yourself, the faster, this is what I hope (laughs), the faster (**Tami:** You're banking on it.) the blessings will come . . .*
>
> ***Abilene:*** *It's a choice (**Bernie:** Well, it's that), yeah, it's adjusting, you have no control of the situation, and maybe you don't have a lot of control, because you're kind of dealt the cards you're dealt. But, it can be how you are reacting to scenarios . . .*

If you've followed any self-help techniques, this should be familiar to you. Control your mind. A difficult situation can be horrible, or it can be a blessing. Change your reactions to situations out of your control. These are great words of wisdom. Apparently, though, they aren't working; otherwise, these precious women wouldn't be as stressed as they are.

So if it's not just the physical, and it's not just the mind—then what else is there? Let's look at the concept of stress as that of a social construct, which may be another new term for you. Only recently have researchers begun looking at stress as something more—something that is constructed in our society through our talk. By *talk*, I mean that which happens on the radio, women's talk shows and magazines, websites, research publications, and talk between and among people. All of this jibber jabber about stress actually creates what stress is. And this babble can be confusing. I did a Google search for "holiday stress women." A well-known online magazine posted an article encouraging women to keep stress from hijacking the holidays. The article warns that stress is caused by the way we think about and function in our environments. *Then* we are encouraged that a few *simple* shifts in thinking can keep stress away. *Oh yay—it's simple!* One groundbreaking idea is to give up perfectionism and the thinking that we *should* do things like make cookies and host parties. Funny thing: on the same page were links to instructions for making your own calendars, holiday food ideas, holiday card ideas, and more. *Now I'm confused. Is stress caused by me doing these things? Not doing these things? Thinking about these things? Are the links there so I'll do things perfectly? Will that decrease my stress? I'm so confused!*

This popular discourse tells us that stress is bad, yet normal; motivating, yet debilitating; universal, yet manageable.

Talking to my friends doesn't really help me either. Some are married with children, have full-time jobs, and come home to messy houses. They always say they're stressed. Others are single full-time students, no kids, and live in apartments. They're all stressed too.

Here's what Bernie says about it:

> *Well, they're already suggesting to the public that we're in a stressed-filled, high-paced, very demanding society, so they have a product that's going to change our life, I guess.*

Oh, this is so powerful, Bernie! Bernie, fifty-five and married, is a full-time librarian with grown children. Her responses were very thoughtful. She seems to get the idea that we're *told* that we are stressed when she uses the vague, unidentified *they*: *They* tell us how stressed we are. *They* show us a society that's worse than it's ever been. And then *they* will sell us a product to fix it. Please don't think of me as conspiracy theorist here—I'm not. But something is going on. Some researchers in this new paradigm claim that in today's world, stress allows someone a certain social standing, almost heroic for those who claim it. These researchers propose, accurately I believe, that stress has now become a way of perceiving the world and as such is of interest to scientists as well as the general public alike.

To understand this, we need to elaborate on my occasional comments about the media. When I say *stress discourse*, I mean those messages that come to us through a variety of sources: through experimental research on stress management, within popular books regarding women's value, and, most recently, within popular women's magazines and books. In both academic and popular discourse, we find commentary about the nature of stress.

Many articles or books claim that too much stress will do you harm. I think we've covered this one pretty well, so enough there. But you'll also find information that tells you stress is inevitable, helpful, and maybe even necessary in life. You know, it's that *we all need a little stress to accomplish things!* Life shouldn't be too easy. Nothing worth accomplishing is ever easy. You gotta buckle down and work hard. This came up occasionally in our conversations.

> ***Dalia:*** *I try not to go to sleep during the day. I am to that point where . . . I now drink caffeine. If I had no responsibilities like that, I would be crazy because I had no responsibilities. I would be looking for responsibilities. I would be looking for those things that cause me stress anyway. Because I have to have something to do. And it has to be something meaningful, it can't be something that has no meaning.*

This was Dalia's reaction after watching the Posturepedic commercial. Dalia interviewed with Lydia, who you met earlier. Like Lydia, Dalia is extremely passionate about her job. Dalia, forty-six and divorced, is a special education teacher. At one point, she referred to herself and Lydia as high achievers. She admits to doing lots of unpaid tasks and even working at night while she talks to her fiancé on the phone. Dalia shared that, even in her sleep, her brain doesn't shut off. Sometimes she wakes up crying and anxious. Hearing this broke my heart. We'll revisit this in chapter 7, but you can see Dalia's description of the necessity of stress—it keeps us going. It's necessary. It's helpful—as long as it's meaningful.

The contradiction of the messages of *stress is good* and *stress is bad* proves that we, society, are creating this conflict and obscuring a real meaning of stress. These messages were present long before stress itself became a major topic of interest for women, yet societal messages continue to be confusing: *Stress is bad and killing us, but it's normal so deal with it. But it's also good, like holiday time. But we should avoid it if we can. But we really can't.* Even the research itself contributes to the social construction of stress and the meanings individuals attribute to it. Stress "experts" in self-help literature, popular magazines, and websites all create this sort of discourse. For example, for women, SuperStay 24 Color by Maybelline® promises women will stay "24 hr. gorgeous . . . even under stress." Ads like this appear in the same publication that tells women how to improve their health by reducing stress.

Earlier I mentioned that, as part of my study, I wanted to include research on stress messages in the media. This type of research is almost nonexistent. The only research I found that directly addresses the issue of stress messages in popular media comes from two fabulous women, Karen Kranz and Bonita Long, dated from 2002. Kranz and Long argue that advertisements encourage consumerism for stress management.[10] Amen! Such marketing techniques present articles that speak to the harmful effects of stress and then supplement that presentation with ads identifying products that will help stressed women feel better. Kranz and Long claim these magazines not only encourage consumerism, they also send the message that women are supposed to change how they think, feel, and behave. Once again I say, Amen!

Let's go further. What do they mean by *messages*? And in what media? Glad you asked. They examined thirty text-only articles from the websites of *Chatelaine* and *Cosmopolitan* magazines. This is certainly a limited study, but at least it suggests that more research is needed. They pointed out two distinct messages about stress. First, stress is universal and unavoidable for women. Second, it is the responsibility of each woman to manage her stress by shopping, seeking advice from experts, and altering her own thoughts, feelings, and behaviors.

They suggested that, for women, stress is caused by taking on too many roles (but, ironically, also too few roles): demanding jobs, having children, driving, caring for parents, balancing demands, and negative thinking, just to name a few. Many of the articles mentioned Harriet Braiker's 1986 Type E woman as a source of stress. The "E" stands for *Everything to Everybody*. These women tend to be perfectionists, have difficulty delegating, and believe they will be liked if they perform well at work and satisfy the needs of others. The Type E woman, like her counterpart Type A man, is at risk for stress-related illness described previously.

The articles supported the perception approaches to stress management we talked about earlier, with advice that women should simply change their thoughts about stress. They encouraged women to purchase a wide variety of products to help with their perceptions: tranquilizers, CDs, aromatherapy products, skin-care products, vitamins, minerals, and a host of other self-help products. One article even proposed a link between modern shopping and our female ancestors' hunt for berries. Apparently, our foremothers got a big thrill from berry hunting, and if we just do some shopping today, we'll get that same thrill and a big stress reduction.

A big boost for these advertisements is that they're often accompanied in the same magazines by credible articles from authorities such as psychiatrists and psychologists. So you have a medical doctor interviewed about how to manage stress, hence: great magazine. Then you have an ad for a product: well, it must be legit if it's in this credible magazine. So women should take this advice and alter the way they think, feel, and behave. This quote came directly from the article—love it!: "Thus, women are not encouraged to use their dis/stress as indicators of legitimate grievances, such as social and contextual factors associated with stress (for ex poverty, poor housing, ill health, poor mgmt. policies, distribution of household/childcare tasks)."[11] Nope—since we just call it stress, there's no need to identify real problems, whether individual or societal.

OK, enough of the soapbox (for now). Kranz and Long's study contributes a great deal to the stress literature as it identifies the importance of how stress is actually perpetuated in women's magazines. They suggest future research should examine how women interpret these messages and how their identities relate to it, which is where my study begins. What I see missing in their analysis and recommendation is the significance of women's conversations in producing this construction.

That's where we will go now. In the next three chapters, we build on our new knowledge that the stressful world we live in might be a lie. We'll find out how these women talked about stress—what words they used. We'll dive deeper into women's conversations. We'll see how we are affected by this culture of stress and then begin to see . . . how to disconnect from the club—forever!

More life advice from real women—Roxy and Mishae:

Roxy: *. . . just knowing that you're never alone, walking with God, even if you can't see him, even if you can't feel him at the time. Just constantly keeping your eyes on the prize, staying focused. Because, you can always stay focused on that, I mean, it will pull you through fire, wind, and rain.*

Mishae: *. . . that is really the main thing that has changed my whole entire life, is just to be in affection with God. And I get in the devotionals when I have problems I can't deal with, or overwhelmed or stressed or something like that but, just God and friends and just trying to stay positive even through all the downs. (**Roxy:** Never give up.)*

Part II:

Participating in the Club

6

Babies, Kittens, and Puppies

Abilene: *Do you know, this dream that I had the other night though, I actually woke up crying! I mean, physically, I was physically crying!* (**Bernie:** *Yeah.*) *In real life. And this was my dream, this will go with your thing, because I know that [having] women in my life [is important] and I have none right now except for at work. I have [none], I know how important that is, because that's when we get to be ourselves. Zero, that's it, period. And so I had this dream that this friend of mine from my last school? She and her daughter were there, her daughter had had something happen to her, we're all kind of talking to it, talking about other things, we were in France for some reason, I don't know why we were there* (**Tami:** *Nice!*)*, but we were just talking and right before I woke up, she and I just embraced, and I just cried on her shoulder, and I woke up missing her so bad, like, I was crying, I was just like "Oh my gosh, I miss my friends."* (**Bernie:** *Awww.*) *Like, because I always knew I could go in [friend's name's] room, [friend's name] is like this goofy, she's one of those people who you know she loves you. Like, there's nothing, and . . . it's this dumb naïve innocent love. It's just the way she is, she's very like "Oh, whatever," you know, about everything. So I knew if I went in her room that she would hug me and I would feel, like, if I was having a bad day, I could always go in her room and she would give me a big hug and ask me how I was* *doing, if she was having a crappy day she'd dump it all on me (laughs), and it would be so funny, yeah. So, honestly, if I had to tell you my biggest stressor right now, is the fact that I am the loneliest freaking lonely I have ever been in my life.*

ISN'T THIS SCRUMPTIOUS AND BEAUTIFUL AND TOUCHING? AND BE HONEST: what would your reaction be if this excerpt came from a man? I'm not saying men are unable to be sensitive or to cry. But most of us would associate this kind of story with women. Is this accurate? Is it fair? I say, absolutely! With some clarification.

Disclaimer: I'm going to say a lot in this chapter about what we do and who we are as women. Please understand, as before, that I'm not saying it's the norm for all of us, but just a pattern with many of us. So not everything I'll say here will apply to you. Okey-dokey? It would take me way too long and way too many words to clarify that after every single point. Also, scientific debates continue on biologically based gender differences. We continue to learn more about our brains and our bodies. I'm not claiming to be an expert in the field of gender biology, so feel free to read further to expand your knowledge. So, onward.

We live in a very complex world today. Gender is actually debated—not the social aspect, but actually *being* male or female. Roles are changing. So let's just get this out of the way—this is not a religious or social debate. I believe we can and *should* discuss differences between females and males. Abilene's words are representative of many women's feelings, of our language, and of our desire to connect—just like we talked about in chapter 4.

I had several goals with my study. One was to discover common ways women talk with one another about stress—recall the interpretative repertoires (themes) I explained in chapter 3. So, how did the women in my study talk about stress as it relates to being a woman? We'll get to that soon, but first we need to talk a bit about us as women—our natures. In high school biology you might have learned about frogs and maybe crayfish and maybe a little about the different kingdoms of life and probably about DNA. You were probably *not* taught specifically about your nature as a woman, how your hormones work, how your body works, and how that relates to your identity.

Perhaps you have never thought about this, but historically, biological research was done on men and used *against* women. In years past, women were viewed simply as smaller versions of men. Our brains, for example, are smaller than men's; how do you think *that* information was used? Yep, it was used to say that we weren't as smart. So it makes sense that women would want to minimize talk about gender differences because that would have been to our detriment. But now we know so much more about biology. Yes, female brains are smaller than men's, but some research finds that every brain cell of a woman is more densely packed with information than a man's. What we lack in size we make up for in efficiency. There's no significant difference in intelligence. There are differences in thinking styles, but not when it comes to intelligence. We are just as smart as men, although you already knew that. So, there you have it—a brief brain lesson.

It is important for you to recognize your biological and chemical makeup before you can understand the nuances of women and stress. It also is important for you to realize how wonderfully and how beautifully created you are. Before you can exit the stress club—and this is the overall goal of this book—you need to understand how your body works. Believe it or not, it will open up your eyes to a whole new world and a whole new attitude, where you can feel proud of how you're made, and also how you can use your nature for your benefit.

Here's a great example: In 2002, a groundbreaking study on stress and how it affects women was published by Shelly Taylor. Prior to about 1995, all stress research was done, as you might have guessed, on men. These researchers came away concluding that all of us, male and female, reacted the same way to a stressful situation: *Fight or Flight.* This happens when a stressful situation comes our way, and we either attack it head-on and deal with it immediately or run away from it and deal with it later. But this new study conducted by Taylor at UCLA discovered a coping mechanism used by many women: *Tend and Befriend.*

Let's talk about the tend part first. If you were with me right now, I would ask you this question: *Do you ever clean or organize or shuffle things or maybe move them around on your desk or your kitchen counter when you're upset?* When I ask this in groups of women, roughly 80 percent or more raise their hands in the affirmative. Next (again, if you were with me) I would ask you: *But how many times have you ever seen a man maybe come in the office or come home and he's had a bad day and he's like, "Give me the vacuum, I've had a bad day!"* I'm gonna say maybe 5 percent of the time, because sometimes men actually do this. This behavior is referred to as tending—our desire to control our environment; sort of like a nesting instinct to keep things in order. So that's the tend part. You might not have known it, but when you are doing this, you are using a mechanism that helps you deal with difficult situations—kudos.

Now let's talk about the befriend half—the *therapy* of talking about it. You've already met Bernie. I love how she talks about girls' night:

> ***Bernie:*** *Well, just to feed back on what you are talking about in terms of having a girls' night, I think that other women and, you know, sisters, whether it's sisters in your family or female friends, they're an incredible amount of support during stressful times, and I don't know where we would be without them. You know, I don't feel like I need medication or a counselor because I feel like that, and you know, those intervening things you do like get out in nature or walk, I mean, all those things that . . . keep you healthy, but emotionally healthy, I think it's having that support of other women.*

What a beautiful description of befriending. *Sisters* who support each other during difficult times. *Not needing* meds or a counselor because of her girlfriends. *Girls' night.* We've all heard the jokes about women—talk, talk, talk—but it's not only *nice* to talk about it, for many of us it is *therapeutic* to talk about it. Whatever *it* is (bosses, employees, friends, spouses, children, etc.). Of course, men, too, probably benefit some from a good vent session, but the research shows that when women tend or befriend, we actually release oxytocin, a feel-good chemical that creates a calming effect. Apparently, men release lots of testosterone when they're stressed, so even though they have oxytocin, testosterone prevents it from having the same effect. Isn't this good information to have?

Back to the study and how these women talked about stress. Meet Carolyn, forty-one, a wife, mother, and teacher. Likewise, meet Rae, fifty, with the same roles as Carolyn's. The three of us were talking about women and stress, and here's how the conversation went:

> ***Carolyn:*** *I think Rae and I are in the real world. I think we are in the real world. (**Rae:** I agree.)*
>
> ***Tami:*** *Which is what?*
>
> ***Rae:*** *I think [the reality is] four to six hours of sleep if you're lucky and the rest of the time you're running nonstop. (**Carolyn:** Yeah.) And I think that's reality.*
>
> ***Carolyn:*** *Mommies don't take days off. (**Tami:** Huh.) So, I think there's a double standard still. You know? It's kind of like the Bible verse where, we were told that we would have pain in childbirth, that was our, you know, punishment for eating the fruit, where men had to toil the ground. Well now, we are toiling the ground and pain in childbirth as far as continuing to have to be mothers constantly, but they didn't have to pick up [anything] extra . . .*

Right? ☺ *We have to do it all now!* Not just *mommies*, but all of us as women in the *real world*. (There's more about the real world in chapter 7). The real world for women, according to Carolyn and Rae, includes luck, double standards, pain, constant running, and picking up and handling all the extras in life. They paint a picture for us that shows women as burdened. Carolyn points out the double standard of roles for men and women. She goes on to describe the biblical concept of punishment for women. Now *that* is certainly a complex topic that I have lots to say about, but it truly is much too complex to address here. Today, Carolyn explains, women are not only punished through childbirth, but also through work. Men, however, have not had to pick up any additional burdens.

By far, the most common theme was that stress was "the plight of women." But it wasn't as simple as just saying, *Yeah, we're women and we're stressed!* It was extremely complex, with deep roots and beliefs about religion, the economy, and our roles as women and as men. We'll see in chapters 9 and 10 that this theme was often at the root of women's stressed-out identities—trying to juggle it all. I quickly noticed two distinct ways they talked about the plight of women.

The first concept of stressfulness as the plight of women was the idea that there are clear societal expectations for us. Most of these women said that the dual roles of modern women cause stress. Many talked about women *now* vs. women *then*. At one point I showed Carolyn and Rae a magazine ad for Relaxity™, an herbal supplement that reportedly causes women to relax. The ad has two cartoon drawings of a woman. The woman on the left hasn't taken the supplement. She's juggling groceries, boxes, and her purse. Her hair's a mess, she's dropped her coffee, and she's rubbing her head as if to say *I've had enough!* The woman on the right is the exact same woman, except she's taken the miracle blend of herbs. She still has the groceries, boxes, coffee, and purse (everything she carried before), but her hair is just perfect, she has a lovely smile on her face, and her coffee is steaming hot. They had this to say:

> ***Carolyn:*** *I think this this reminds me of the fifties.* (Woman on the right in the ad)
>
> ***Rae:*** *On* Leave It to Beaver–*June.*
>
> ***Carolyn:*** *Yeah, the things they just did. We are expected to go to work and do everything at work; this is the 2012 woman. You know? Where we are doing everything.* (Woman on the left)

So earlier they talked about the burdens of women and here they follow up with a comparison of the women of yesteryear who had limited responsibilities, while women of today must do *everything.*

Ahhh, if we could only go back to June Cleaver's time—or do we *really* want that? As we've discussed before, just because a woman has a smile on her face doesn't necessarily mean she's happy.

Recall Abilene and Bernie, very busy women in the world today. During our discussions about women and stress, I also showed them the ad for Relaxity. Remember the picture of the woman *without* this miracle extract looks a mess. Here's what they said about her:

> ***Abilene:*** *She's disorganized, she's a big mess, look at her hair, she hasn't brushed her hair, she doesn't care about what she looks like, because she doesn't have time to care about what she looks like . . .*
>
> ***Bernie:*** *Well, she's got worries on her mind, and she can't focus, she's dropping things (**Tami:** Okay.), she's not able, and just the visual, she's not able to balance it all. She can't balance everything that's in her life.*

They both refer to the inability of women to do it all, with Bernie using the word *can't* twice, along with *not able.* Both women were very passionate about the issue of balance, and Abilene places strong emphasis on the word *time.* Here, women are seen as lacking choice and control over stress, as presumed from how they use terms and phrases such as *can't* and *not able.* Other women also used descriptors such as *too much*, and *that's part of it for women.*

I'm guessing you may have identified with these women. We seem to have so many expectations placed on us today in the twenty-first century. Bring home the bacon, fry it up in a pan . . . never forget your man . . . blah, blah, blah! It wasn't just the women's words you see here. It was all of the women I talked with. Think about your conversations with your friends, family, and coworkers. How many times have you said or heard comments about all that women have to do? In chapter 5, Pebbles described it as *so overwhelming that . . . you just kind of, like, fold and collapse and give up.*

A second way they talked about stress as a woman's plight focuses more on the innate nature of our emotions and feelings. This was such a deep, emotional concept, so I'm including several women here. I want you to *feel* what they're saying. You've met Phoebe and Kay. Let's *listen in* on what they say about our nature:

Tami: *Well, let me ask you this, because you talked about your husbands and you talked about racquetball, do you think that it's just, like, normal for women to be stressed-out? Is that, like, a normal state today? In society?*

Phoebe: *I feel like, yeah.*

Kay: *Mm-hmm, oh, yeah. I'm telling you, my mother-in-law once told me, she said, "You know, being a woman's never fair. It's not right, but that's the way God made it and that's just that's the way it is." You know, we were discussing the responsibilities of a woman, and the mothering, and the being a wife, and all the roles that you take on, it's just, it's not right, but that's just the way it is, . . .*

Phoebe: *Yeah. Yeah, I would say that. Probably.*

Wow! It's not right. It's not fair. But it's just the way it is. It's the way we're made. In contrast to the first way of talking about women—societal expectations—this way drills down to our very makeup. *Now I'm* really *feeling like there's no hope.* Of course, there is hope. This is why I so desperately want women to have a new view of stress.

Remember Jacqueline and Grace, our soul sisters?

Tami: *So do you think it's worse for women than it is for men? Like, when we talk about stress. (**Jacqueline:** Yeah.) (**Grace:** Yes.)*

Jacqueline: *I mean, it's not like they don't carry some of the same amount of stress that we do, but we just take it, we take it so much more to heart, I think, than they do.*

Tami: *Different stressors and just different reactions and? (**Jacqueline:** Mm-hmm.)*

Grace: *Yeah, my husband's okay if the house was messy, you* *know. And as a mom, I feel like I'm kind of a failure if people come to my house. I don't think he sees it that way (**Tami:** Right.), but I feel less than, you know (**Jacqueline:** Right.), if I have dishes in the sink or something like that . . .*

That feels like a fairly accurate perception, right? Oftentimes men don't seem to be all freaked out by a messy house. They don't seem to carry around stress like we do. We take things to heart. In a nutshell, we just *feel* things more. I'm going to agree with that. With a *but . . . Is it inevitable?*

You've seen part of this before from Erica, but I've added more here:

***Erica:** I think, and we kind of talked about this before you got here, when my girlfriends and I get together we all absolutely talk openly about the stresses of day-to-day life, and I do think it is pretty much the norm. I was trying to think when you said that when the last time I felt like I wasn't stressed-out, and I don't really know when that was, but I will say my husband on the other hand (laughs), he doesn't seem to be stressed ever. And his job is, I mean, to me? From the outside looking in looks very stressful to me. But he just takes it in a different way. I feel like women almost harbor it and don't, I don't know.*

So women talk. Stress is the norm. Men have stress, too. Maybe the same. Maybe more. But they don't seem to get stressed like we do. We seem to *harbor* it! Again. Agree. *But, again . . . is it inevitable?*

Finally, one more. You've already met Rae, but not Ginger (these are two separate interviews). Ginger, forty-three and married, is a full-time teacher. Her heart seems to be for her family, and she focuses a great deal of her talk on how they are affected both by her and by the world in general. Rae is talking about teacher evaluations and the times when state evaluators just drop in unexpected. Here are their thoughts on our nature:

***Rae:** I know that we need to get our scores up and get education up, but the fact that they drop in, women automatically*

> *worry anyway? I think, maybe I'm speaking just for myself, but, I can name I don't know how many female friends here that we have all cried with each other and panicked going, "Oh, my gosh, they're coming in, they're coming in" and we plan lessons every day, but to have someone analyze and write every word that you say down . . .*
>
> ***Ginger:** I think it's going to get worse simply just because the world continues on a downward spiral. I think it's just, that's the reason I think it's going to get worse. And probably not only for women. I know primarily that's what we're talking about, but I think it's just going to get bad for everybody. And women often take the brunt, . . . we're such emotional creatures and we think that we have to fix stuff, but I think oftentimes we take the brunt of stuff. . . for things that happen to our families, for things that happen to our jobs, to our careers, you know, we take a lot of that in and we feel a lot of that blame and we try to shoulder that (**Tami:** Take it to heart.) (**Ginger:** Mm-hmm.) We try to shoulder that and. . . it's not always our responsibility to do that.*

The visuals here are powerful: crying, panicking, worrying, taking the brunt, being emotional, wanting to fix, feeling blame, shouldering responsibility. You've probably done or felt all of these things, and maybe you're a little tired of it. It's interesting how Ginger says conditions in the world are going to get worse for men as well, and then describes why it matters more for us as women. Keep hope—we're working on it!

In all of these conversations, men and women are contrasted in regard to how they handle stress. Most of them admitted that men also have stress in their lives, sometimes more so than women. What is different, they claim, is how women deal with it. Kay describes women under the Christian belief that God made us that way, referring to the multiple responsibilities women must shoulder. Erica refers to how women *harbor it.* Both women used lots of metaphors to describe the nature of women such as *internalize it,* and *We take it so much more to heart.* Often these were used in direct contrast to men, who are able to let things go. You probably already agree that they're right—that we do take things to heart more. Feel more. Carry more. But is it a biological issue?

To explore this, let's revisit our earlier discussion of women and biology and consider this question—one that leads to lots of conversation: *What do you consider to be the traditional role of a man?* I often ask this question during sessions on stress, emotions, or balance, and I've asked it all over the United States, Australia, New Zealand, and the United Kingdom. With few exceptions, I'd say 90 percent of the time I get these answers: *provider*, *protector*, *defender*. You might be nodding your head in agreement (or disagreement). I understand that men's roles have changed some; sometimes men stay home and take care of children. But do we still expect them to fulfill that traditional role? Think about this: You see a man, and he doesn't work. What do you think about him? The words I usually hear are *irresponsible*, *loser*, *slacker*. So would you say that we still expect men to fulfill traditional roles? Many of us, in terms of conventional expectations, expect men to work, especially if they have a family—to provide for their family. Do you think a man is biologically set up to do this? In other words, does he have special physical characteristics that equip him to do this?

If we think about a man as protector and defender, we have to go back a bit in history to the time of hunting, killing, protecting the cave—you know, that kind of thing. Think about muscle mass, which is greater in men than in women. Think about the primary sex hormone that men have, testosterone. We, too, have testosterone, but men have it in higher quantities. It's the chemical that can lead to more aggressive tendencies. Does it make sense that a man is biologically wired to go out and hunt the deer, kill the deer, and drag the deer home? It seems so, right? Also, the structures of the brain—the areas of the brain associated with aggressive tendencies and sex drive—are larger in the male brain. That seems right as well, doesn't it? I know most men, at least here in the United States, no longer have to hunt and kill to provide for their families, but I hope you get my point: there are biological structures associated with being a man. And there are reasons for these structures.

Let's ask the same type of question about women: *What would you consider the traditional role of a woman to be?* Again, I ask this question all the time, and again, 90 percent of the time the responses are fairly traditional: *nurturer, caretaker, homemaker.*

Have women's roles changed? Of course, just like men's roles have. Actually, women's roles have changed more than men's. Recall what these women have shared with you: It seems that not only are we expected to be the nurturer, caretaker, and homemaker, but we're also expected to work. Think about this situation: Let's say there's a husband and wife, and they have two children. He works full-time and takes care of the family as much as he can, but they're headed toward financial disaster and possibly bankruptcy. The mom, the wife, makes the choice to still stay home with the children. What do people say about her? *She should get off her behind and get a job.* You met Jackie when I introduced this comment in our chapter 3 intro:

> ***Jackie:*** *I almost think that's one of the negatives of being a woman, is that there's expectations, even if your husband does DO childcare or housework, I think a woman still has the overarching responsibility. And so we have that task, domestic and relational and social. You know, my husband's not out making Thanksgiving plans or making sure our Christmas cards are going to get sent out. (laughs) You know, so we're dealing with all that on top of work and that's what's I think more challenging.*

Jackie, like the others, talks about these negatives as part of *being*. Are our difficulties biologically inevitable?

Here we go with the same biology question I asked about men: Are our bodies biologically set up to be the nurturer? Our bodies are set up to bear children. Now, whether you have children or not is not the point, but the setup is there, right? I obviously do not believe we're all just baby machines; I have both a career and a family. But the fact is the female gender got the ovaries, which makes the egg. We got the uterus, the little pouch to carry it around; we even got mammary glands to nourish the child. So doesn't it make sense, even to those who can't or don't have children, that if our bodies are equipped to produce, carry, deliver, and nourish children, that we also should have some structures and chemicals that enable us to care for and teach them? As much as we might want a father to be present, that doesn't always happen. So we've got some characteristics that enable us to take care of those children. Understanding this will help you process some of the reasons behind the idea of stress as the plight of women. Let's talk about the female brain.

We said that male brains are larger, but every little cell inside of the female's brain is more densely packed with information. Women have more neurons in our language and hearing centers. Doesn't that make total sense? We need to be the ones who can communicate, because if we have the capacity to have a child, we should certainly have the ability to pass on information. So it's probably not a surprise to you that we have a larger communication center than men do. Our hippocampus, which is the section of the brain responsible for connecting emotions and memory, is larger in the female brain and this is why you'll hear, or you might say something like, maybe to your husband or to another man, *Remember when you said that you liked my hair, but you liked it better when it was blonde? Remember that? Like six months ago? That hurt my feelings.* Yeah, you've probably done something like this before! We create deep memories when it comes to emotional experiences.

Here are a few more tidbits, little interesting facts about your brain: Your frontal lobe is more active than a man's, which means that you think through consequences more carefully and you tend to be a more effective writer. Your occipital lobe, which controls vision, is more active, and that allows you to see better in dim light. This also allows you to read emotions better on other people's faces, even in low light. This is partly why you are more likely than a man to say, *I saw that look on her face. I saw that look on his face.*

Your parietal lobe, which is responsible for touch and pain, is more active than a man's, so you feel pain more fully. (You might already realize this.) This enhanced sensitivity also means you might enjoy longer hugs and other types of physical contact. You've probably seen teenage girls sit on each other's laps, braid each other's hair, and put their arms around each other. I'm curious how we'd respond if we saw teenage boys do that (another example of our expectations, and it is evidence that we really do recognize that there are gender differences). Your temporal lobe, which is responsible for hearing, is more active. This is the reason, just like that whole thing about *I saw that look on your face*, that you're more likely to say, *Well, I heard that tone in your voice!* We pick up on these things more often than men.

Overall, research tells us that our brains don't really turn off. They're always working in a million different ways, and they crave activity. And many researchers believe that intimacy and relationships are very challenging activities and, in ways, are most productive for your brain, and that's why we work on these things so much.

Let's move on from the brain and talk about some of the chemicals. We talked about the primary sex hormone in men being testosterone and how that led to those aggressive tendencies among males. Let's talk about two chemicals we women have. The first one, which you probably know about and love, is estrogen. Let's hear again from Roscoe, who, at fifty-three, presumably has ample experience with some seasons of life and hormones.

> ***Roscoe:*** *Now, I'll tell you another thing is getting older and the hormone levels and perimenopause, tell you what, that has, is causing stress. (laughs)*
>
> ***Tami:*** *So that for women (**Roscoe:** Yes.) has an effect.*
>
> ***Roscoe:*** *Yes, absolutely. Because my doctor . . . he says, "We're going to fix you. Let me tell you about you, this is what you're like." He says, "You're like the plane that's coming in for a landing, but you're bumping around, you know," that's how he describes perimenopause, because that's where I'm at. He says, "But once you land, you're going to be fine, you know, but we just need to get you landed and stuff" and . . . (laughs) (**Tami:** I like that analogy.) Yeah, it makes sense, that's true. But, it has been very difficult and stressful, dealing with hormones and what it does to your body. (**Bessie and Tami:** Yeah.) (laughs) Yes.*

Ahhhh, estrogen! Notice both Bessie and I agree with Roscoe, and we laugh! Estrogen is the primary female sex hormone and it gives us some of the symptoms of—you might have heard of it—PMS, and there's another one called PMDD, Premenstrual Dysphoric Disorder. PMDD is like PMS on steroids, so it's more descriptive of the mood changes than anything else, and there's actually medication for it. Here's the thing: the science of emotions is not as exact as many other sciences involving the systems of your body. When you go to the doctor and get your cholesterol drawn, your doctor might say, *OK, if it's over this number, then you need to be on medication or change your diet.* When it comes to emotions, though, some things are just not quite as clear.

Here's what some research suggests: during this period of time that we call PMS, or premenstrual syndrome, estrogen levels drop. When levels drop, a neurotransmitter called serotonin also drops. A neurotransmitter is simply a chemical in your brain that allows your cells to keep contact with one another; you need a high-enough level for your own body to keep your emotions in check. So serotonin drops when estrogen drops, and what you feel is a real chemical change going on inside of your brain. Like Roscoe, I'm also in the stage called perimenopause. Maybe you are familiar with this, but it's the period of time where you're still having periods, but you're beginning to have those hot flashes and extreme mood swings as well.

Story time. My husband and I had been invited to a football game—actually to sit in a stadium suite! It was a beautiful day; there was food, lots of fun, music, laughter. We were sitting with some other people, and I mentioned to him that I might want to do some volunteering at the kids' school. He said *OK*, and then turned around and proceeded to talk to somebody else. I sat there for a couple minutes and felt my blood pressure start to rise. My muscles tensed. My face got hot, and my heart was pounding! Before I knew it, I ran out of that suite in tears—I could *not* compose myself because I could not believe that he would not have a longer conversation with me than that! When those things happen to me I have to take a step back and say, *OK, could this be distorted? Could there be a chemical change going on that is causing me to react in a way that I might not normally react?* And I'm saying this to you because we get so irritated and defensive about those PMS jokes (which, granted, they're *not* always funny), but if we recognize it, we're able to change our reactions to other people during those times when maybe, just maybe, we're not completely ourselves. We'll revisit this in chapter 12 when you create your exit strategy.

So there you go, a little bit about me and a lot about estrogen. Now let's talk about one other chemical that affects your emotions and how you feel. That's oxytocin. I'll explain it to you in terms of a video I sometimes show during women's conferences. It's called *Gizmo's First Bark*. Gizmo is a little black and white Shih Tzu puppy, a precious little ball of fur, playing by a full-length mirror on the wall. Gizmo runs over to it, but he gets confused because there's another image there, and he thinks it's another dog. So he runs toward it and runs back and runs toward it and runs back—over & over. Finally, he gets up the nerve, runs at his image, bangs into the mirror, and lets out a bark. That really scares him, and he falls over and rolls down a step. When I show this video to a group of women, what do you think I hear? Well, if you said *Awww*, then you're right. I hear a lot of *Awwws* in the room. Now think about this: what if you were walking down a hotel hallway and you happened to peek into a room full of men in a seminar, and *they're* watching this video, and you hear them all go *Awww*? What would you think? I mean, as before, I'm not making a judgment, I'm just saying it might be different. It just doesn't happen that often, as the reaction has a chemical component.

Oxytocin is the *Awww* hormone. It's the maternal bonding hormone. It's the reason that women often feel a different type of emotion when they see babies and kittens and puppies. Most men, if I showed them that video, might laugh and think it's funny, or they might say something like "stupid dog" or hit the guys next to them. So it's interesting to me to listen to some of the issues that women bring up, especially when I teach a seminar about balance. I once had a woman throw her hand up in irritation (you can always just bet that person is going to have an interesting question when that hand just *flings* up!). She threw up her hand and said, *You know, it just really bugs me that every time my son has a problem at school or he gets sick, the school always calls me, they never call his dad.* So I said to her, *Well, they call you because you'll actually show up!* I don't mean to dog on men here, but we hear the jokes all the time—men just don't respond as quickly or as well as women do to relationship issues. The joke isn't always true, but remember: doesn't it make sense (we've used that phrase many times) that if we have the capacity to bear children, that we're going to have some hormones that give us an increased awareness to them? Now you may be thinking, *My husband has more maternal tendencies than me!* That may be absolutely true. As I mentioned before, these behaviors are patterns, not norms. I bring this up because I see the agony in some of these young moms when they leave their babies at six weeks. Who came up with six weeks? That's forty-two days, when a mother has carried this little fetus around for nine months, given birth, and forty-two days later she's supposed to make the break. It can be tough when oxytocin wants you to bond, and society says you need to cut loose.

Again, I'm not saying that we shouldn't work or we should go back to the barefoot and pregnant days. I just want to point out there are chemical reasons for the way we feel, and that we do have a relationship chemical. Even if you don't have children now, or even if you never have children, you still have oxytocin that affects your bonding and attachment to other people, as well as to children. Maybe you are a young mother or mother-to-be, or maybe you know a young mother or mother-to-be, or maybe you just desire more relationships with other people. Understand that oxytocin is there for you. It is triggered by hugging, when we experience intimacy, when we shop, and when we gossip (maybe not the best example!). And it makes us feel good, and that's the whole point of talking about this. It's a chemical that makes us feel good; it makes our brains feel alive.

So that's estrogen and oxytocin, what they do to your body and how they make you feel.

So back to the question: *Is it inevitable that stress is the plight of women?* We've spent a lot of time on this, but it's so important, considering *all* of the women talked about stress this way. This indicates there must be characteristics, traits, etc., specific just to us. And there are. We do have the biology that predisposes us to caring and nurturing. But of course there's more to it than just biology. We live in a society that oftentimes still places unrealistic expectations on us, stemming from culture, religion, or family values. Recall the Happiness Formula we talked about in chapter 2. Genetics is part of it. Conditions of life are part of it. But most importantly, remember the value of voluntary activities. We are women, and we should become women of power and women of choices! That's what the exit strategy will focus on in chapter 12, but we still have more to cover. Next, let's look at conversations about stress as part of living in the real world.

More life advice from real women–Jacqueline and Grace:

Jacqueline: *Don't compare yourself to others. . . . I see other women, just like that ad that you showed me, that seem to have, like, the really nice handbag and their clothes look nicer and their makeup looks nice and their little kids and their pretty little Chico stroller and they just seem like they have it so much more together. And then I'm frumpy in my jeans and sweatshirt and like, well, how come I don't look like that, how come I don't, how come I feel more frazzled than she looks, you know? But, like, her husband could be cheating on her. Like, he could be a real jerk. And mine's sweet and helpful. Like, I don't know anything about her (**Grace:** Right.) and what she's carrying, like, I'm wasting so much emotional energy worrying about what other people are doing or how, instead of trying to just be the best me that I can be . . . I'm going to take my own damn advice this week (laughs) and, so I would just say let go of the guilt and stop comparing yourself to other people. Because you don't know.*

Grace: *I think just carving out some quiet time. I think that's been the . . . thing that's helped me sort of discover who I am again after kids. You know, because I think it takes me a few years after I have a child to kind of concentrate on myself again? So, as much quiet time or, you know, working out would be ideal. That's what I would say to handle a lot of stress, but at least some time where you can enjoy something that you enjoy.*

7

Occasional Sprinkles of Fairy Dust

Tami: *Tell me, what does that mean, like, when you hear "in the real world," what is that? Like, what you think the real world is. Have you said it before? (***Jacqueline:** *Mm-hmm.)*

Grace: *. . . "Well, in my world," you know. (laughs)*

Tami: *Okay, oh, right, or something like that, yeah, what would that mean? Like, what you think that that's all about.*

Grace: *Well, I guess people like that lady [in mattress commercial] don't really live in the real world? Because they don't have to deal with daily stress, you know? They have housekeepers and people working for them and take on so many of the stresses.*

Jacqueline: *And if they do feel stressed, they have time, they can afford to pay to get a massage. Or a facial. Or a pedicure. Like, those luxuries like those beauty luxuries, I feel like that's one of the things that I'm most jealous of. If I see a woman who looks pretty and put together, then I'm just like, well, you know, she doesn't work where I work or (laughs) (***Grace:** *Right) . . . you know, she doesn't. . .*

Grace: *She's not working full-time with kids at home, that's for sure.*

Jacqueline: *Yeah . . .*

Grace: *That's the real world. (laughs)*

YOU PROBABLY REMEMBER JACQUELINE AND GRACE, OUR SOUL SISTERS! And you've likely been a part of this type of conversation before: *the real world!* The lady they're referring to is the woman in the Sealy Posturepedic mattress commercial we discussed in chapter 1. It was part of Sealy's *Get a Better Six* campaign. I think at this point it's a good idea to show you the transcript. (You can also watch for yourself at https://www.youtube.com/watch?v=Q7ShnNPWvbs,) The ad depicts a woman who has apparently married a wealthy man. The spokesperson says:

> *Meet Judith Goldbrush, gold digger. She spends like there's no tomorrow; she also sleeps like there's no tomorrow. Ah, wedded bliss. But what about the rest of us? In the real world, we're lucky to get six hours of sleep. So, let's get a better six.*

Every time I showed this commercial in my seminars and in my study, *robust* conversations ensued as women gave their assessments of Mrs. Gold Digger. They did not like Mrs. Judith Goldbrush! I saw this ad several years ago while I was teaching for Skillpath Seminars—I was so intrigued. I wondered what advertisers meant by the *real world*, so I discussed it with women who attended my stress seminars.

We would talk about it for a bit. They would express their disgust. They would scoff, roll their eyes, and nudge their friends and laugh. So after a bit of that I would ask them to raise their hands if *they* got adequate sleep on a fairly regular basis. You might recall in chapter 1 I already told you the outcome of this question: never have I had a lone woman raise her hand.

I actually saw a little of myself in these women, and I wondered about my own responses to these advertisements. I thought about times I was reluctant to tell a friend I had slept in or relaxed for the day. I remember calling my sister one Sunday, and she told me she had been up since six that morning. *Six o'clock?! Is it even* light *out at six?!* I asked. Then, without thinking, I added, *Well, I was up at six, but we have room-darkening curtains.* She went on to say *she* was *always* up at six. Then I said *I* was *always* up at six too. Then we talked about how much we had to do: our houses were too messy, our kids were too demanding, our husbands weren't helpful, and how we would never be able to get everything done! We laughed. We huffed and puffed. Oh, we were absolutely sure our lives were out of control. Funny thing: when I thought back on it, I realized I *wasn't* up at six! Furthermore, I don't *always* get up at six, and I know she doesn't *always* get up at six, so what the heck? At the time, I was a Platinum Member of the Stress Club. I'm not discounting the challenges we both had as wives and mothers, but the fact is we used our language to accomplish something other than reflecting what time we always got up. As women, we used our words to ensure identities of responsibility and to bond over our mutual suffering in the real world. We were both in the club. These reflections were difficult, as I realized I, too, was saying so many of the same things I had heard from other women. This is why I included the ad in my study.

Let me backpedal to the outcomes of my study. We discovered in the last chapter that one theme women used while chatting was stress as the *plight* of women. Although that theme involves societal expectations of women, both now and in times past, this next theme identifies stressfulness as a direct result of living in the *real world.* This is the world that includes technology, the media, the economy, family, work, and today's value systems. When these ladies heard of lives they perceived as happy or low stress, they characterized those lives as *fiction, fantasy world, and dream land.*

They talked about the real world in three ways, all intertwined to a degree. One way was through descriptions of society in general. Women most often used this approach when asked if it was normal to be stressed-out in today's society.

Meet Lily and Claire. Lily, forty-four and married, is a stay-at-home mom; Claire, fifty-five, is a married teacher with grown children. These were the only two women in my study who didn't know each other before the interview, so that was fun! Of course, I wasn't studying the differences between friends' conversations versus the conversations of strangers, but I could hear, see, and feel that it was different. After showing the mattress commercial to Lily and Claire, I asked them if it's normal to be stressed-out today. Here's what they said:

Tami: *Well, do you think that it's just a normal state today then, to just be stressed-out?*

Claire: *Yeah (laughs).*

Lily: *I think more so in this generation (**Tami:** Really?) (**Claire:** I do.) than ever before because there's just so many things going on and . . .*

Claire: *Well, we're too accessible, I think is a huge problem. With instant messaging and phone and the Internet.*

Lily: *The Internet.*

Claire: *The phone especially.*

Lily: *Oh, I think we're just too accessible, therefore we're always on. There's no downtime. (**Tami:** Hmm.)*

Claire: *Absolutely.*

One more excerpt and then I'll break them down. You've met Bessie before. Same question—here's what she said:

Bessie: *I think everybody's much too busy with way too many places to go and be and the whole can't get away from your phone (**Roscoe** and **Tami:** Mm-hmm.), can't get away from your computer, can't get away from, I don't know, all these distractions that keep you from interacting with people.*

They all talked about how society today is an unavoidably busy, fast-paced environment. Lily and Claire blame the Internet and phones for making us too accessible. Oh, curse you, Facebook! And Twitter! And Instagram! (Actually, I love all that stuff. And my son works for Facebook, so I'd better love it.) Bessie strongly believes that women can't get away from today's distractions and that those intrusions actually interfere with relationships. That's a serious situation. Many of the other women also talked about the lack of choices regarding today's technology, i.e., *It's just part of the world today and I have no choice but to participate twenty-four hours a day.* Some described it as an *addiction.* Others said they thought it had a negative effect on the family structure. Similar to the *woman's plight*, there was a lot of talk about lack of choice. It makes me sad when I hear women say they feel trapped, without choice.

None of this is a surprise to you, right? Sit at the dinner table with your family. Go to the store. Walk down the street. Everyone's on their phones. And we think it's just youngsters, but not anymore. Recently, in a diner in Hershey, Pennsylvania, I sat next to a couple in their seventies (my assumption). We were sitting there for about a half-hour, and they were both on their phones the entire time. They were talking, but not to each other. So it seems we're always available, in diners, stores, at work, in bed, and now even on airplanes. But is it a choice? We'll delve into this more in a bit and also when you create your exit strategy in chapter 12.

Another time the *real world* theme reared its ugly head was in response to a vignette about a fictitious, but based-on-real-life, woman named Samantha. I actually opened up the study with this little story:

> *Samantha is very happy with her life. She is married with two children. Her husband shares the housework and childcare duties. She works part-time and her schedule is flexible. Her boss is very understanding, and she gets along well with her coworkers.*

At that point I asked the women to share their initial thoughts about Samantha's life. Before I show you what they said, let me tell you why I used this story. For several years prior, I had been teaching numerous managing-emotions classes all across the United States, the United Kingdom, Australia, and New Zealand. The last time I went to Australia before going back to school, I decided to gather some informal data. I used this scenario, and let me just tell you, these people did *not* like Samantha! I actually had them write down their reactions, and I thought you'd like to see a summary of them. (Since there were more than three hundred, I didn't think you'd want to see them all.)

Out of ~ 340 responses,

48 of them had the word *lucky*. That's 14 percent.

4 fortunate

8 jealous

4 envious

8 wish (meaning they *wished* they had Samantha's life)

16 had "Good on him" (In Australia, they often say *good on* instead of *good for*), "Good for Samantha," "Good for you," etc. (Not all, by the way, were sarcastic. Some were genuinely happy for Samantha. I knew this after our follow-up discussions.)

6 "too good to be true" statements

10 denial

2 antidepressants (meaning Samantha must be on them!)

4 dream/dream land

3 rubbish

4 not true

3 liar

5 crap

2 lying

4 untrue

5 unrealistic

1 not reality

Some of them actually cursed—I left those off. But I felt like I had hit a nerve and that it would be a great way to kick off these conversations about stress.

OK, back to our ladies. Before I give you a very detailed conversation, I'm just going to give you a list of the comments, and you'll notice the similarity to what I'd already heard. I loved this part of the study—just because it was so telling of how we feel about the real world. Take a look:

Claire: *Must be nice. (laughs)*

Lily: *Sounds like dream world. (laughs)*

Jackie: *Oh, I think spoiled in a good-humored sense. (laughs)*

Jacqueline: *Well, Samantha's hilarious. (laughs) Samantha's got it all, doesn't she? Yeah.*

Grace: *That's what I think, too. My first thought is that's kind of not fair. (Laughs) That she works part-time and gets all that extra help?*

Mishae: *Blessed, wow.*

Roxy: *Lucky.*

Dorian: *Seems very ideal. (**Tami:** Seems ideal?) Almost like utopia. Like, unreal.*

Erica: *I was thinking unreal as well.*

Ginger: *I would like to be Samantha. (Laughs)*

Candy: *It sounds like she's got a pretty good setup.*

After hearing about Samantha's life, most of the women talked about the good life as unachievable. Nearly all of these sweet women argued that someone appearing to live a low-stress, happy life is hiding something. Lots of laughter and nudging. Their voices got louder. Lots of disbelief. Eye-rolling. They just weren't buying it—that's not the real world! No *way* can someone live like that! There's more here than just the real world stuff, and we'll come back to this in chapters 10 and 11. I want to present one detailed conversation before we leave Samantha. Recall Abilene and Bernie. Abilene is quite passionate about the concept of real life:

Abilene: *She's fiction.*

Tami: *She's fiction?*

Bernie: *Yeah, I was going to say fairy tale.*

Tami: *Fairy tale. Okay. Now, tell me why. Like, expand on that a little bit.*

Abilene: *(Psht)*

Tami: *Did you go "Psht"?*

Abilene: *Yeah.*

__Tami:__ Okay.

__Abilene:__ Well, first of all, it—life isn't like that. I mean, it isn't always like, maybe it's like that for her, maybe that's a snapshot of her life and everything just hap——, the stars aligned for her at that moment? (__Tami:__ Okay.) But that means that tomorrow something terrible is going to happen. (laughs) (__Tami:__ Okay.) True? I mean, really, so. Her boss is going to retire and a new boss is going to come in who's a big jerk or doesn't care for her or is a different kind of leadership style that doesn't agree with necessarily her personality type. . . . I have seen two research studies done recently about husbands. On one hand, it said husbands are happier if they take part in the housework, another one said that they're happier if they aren't. How in the world? (__Tami:__ So what's up with that?) Yeah, it's bull, is what it is.

Abilene's words are especially powerful. Like many women, she says that life can be happy as a snapshot, but that something bad will inevitably happen. Then she provided a detailed outline of the possible tragedies that might befall Samantha. She looked to Bernie and me for confirmation, saying, *Right?* Abilene expresses what many women seem to be feeling: the real world is not kind, even if it is occasionally sprinkled with fairy dust.

The final talk about being stressed-out as obligations of the real world came, as did the first way, after viewing the mattress commercial and asking the question, *What is the real world?* Here, the answers contained lots of descriptions of life as being hard and full of obligations, as you'll see here from Roscoe and Bessie, and Jackie and Sondra.

__Roscoe:__ Work and family.

__Bessie:__ Yeah. And I guess, too, when you're actually experiencing life and not in a fantasy. Like she was having this, obviously, some sort of fantasy of just pamperment and, luxury, and that's not the real world. Like we are obviously not in that world, but. . .

Roscoe: *Yeah, not at all, I guess, yeah.*

Bessie: *. . . in the real world, what does that mean? Work, family time, being responsible for yourself and your family.*

Jackie: *Hard. Maybe life is hard.*

Sondra: *I mean, most of us aren't representative of the lady in that commercial (**Jackie:** Yeah.) and her life.*

Tami: *So most of us have . . .*

Jackie: *A majority.*

Sondra: *We work. We have to get up for work. (**Tami:** Okay.), we have . . .*

Jackie: *Bills to pay.*

Sondra: *Bills to pay, you know, lots of things that we have to do before we can go to bed, and then to have to get up the next morning even if we didn't sleep well.*

Tami: *Even if you don't want to. (**Sondra:** Even if we don't want to, yeah.) If you didn't sleep well. Okay.*

So the real world is hard with so many responsibilities. We have to go to work, fulfill family obligations, pay bills, and sometimes not get enough sleep. Bessie described the real world as living outside of a fantasy. Sondra and Jackie discussed what makes life hard, and Sondra ended with, *have to get up the next morning even if we didn't sleep well.* Other women described financial burdens and living in the world today meant having to *make things happen* in contrast to the woman in the commercial. So we need to be responsible no matter what life throws at us.

I made the point when we talked about being stressed as a woman's plight that it was probably no surprise to you. And I'll say the same thing here. None of these conversations made you gasp in shock and horror! You've heard them and probably been a part of them. Life is hard. Real life isn't fun. People with simple lives are hiding something or financially blessed or on the verge of some tragedy. Life is stressful. So *is* society more stressful today than ever before? *Are* we at the mercy of the real world? Let's see what Erica thinks:

> ***Erica:*** *I don't know, because listening to my grandmother and my mom talk, I think they definitely had stresses. You know, [my grandmother] going through the Great Depression, my mom was a single mom for a time with my brother and I think it was different stresses, I think society just seems faster now. And maybe stressful for different reasons, but I feel like my grandmother, even though she stayed at home having six kids, that to me sounds like a nightmare. And having to do it all and to have a façade and to be ready when my grandfather got home and to look as if it was easy, I mean, I don't think that sounds fun at all? And then my mom having to do it on her own and then have the scarlet letter of being a single parent and getting a divorce and she actually got pregnant before she was married so that's a whole other thing. So I think the same kind of stresses have always been there, but I just think it's faster now. I still think, I mean, I don't know that I would trade with my grandmother or my mom, but I still think they had stresses, I just think it's different.*

So Erica says that maybe we aren't *more* stressed today, just *differently* stressed. I totally identified with Erica here when it comes to the difficulties of staying home with six kids. I loved staying home with my three when they were little, but to be essentially forced into it? To have the expectation that when Daddy gets home I'd better have it all together—clean, well-behaved children, dinner on the table and a cute little party dress on? I gotta tell you, after reading Betty Friedan's book, *The Feminine Mystique*, I am pretty grateful for my life as a woman today, at least her in the U.S. Maybe you lived the life of a 1950s housewife. If not, maybe you've experienced it by watching *Mad Men*.

So home life has changed, and depending on what you value you could say it is *more* stressful or *less* stressful (hating the word *stressful*, of course). What about work life? Much has changed in how we work over the years, and trends and desires have been documented. According to the Economic History Association (2010), the number of hours worked in America has actually decreased by about 30 percent since the 1800s. Prior to the Industrial Revolution, most agricultural work was done on a seasonal, sun-up to sun-down basis, sometimes entailing twelve hours a day for six months out of the year. The first enforceable hours' law in the United States was in 1874, when Massachusetts enacted a law limiting the number of hours that women and children could work each week to sixty. Men were not covered under any work laws at this time, the rationale being they could negotiate for themselves.

The average workweek by the 1920s was fifty hours, and by 1927 many organizations had adopted the five-day workweek. Work hours in the twenty-first century continue to fluctuate for many reasons, including the economy, war, automation, and even media messages. Interestingly, even as the five-day, forty-hour workweek gained popularity, many opposed further shortening of the workweek. Many researchers talk about workers living under what was called the *gospel of consumption*, the belief that more work led to more money led to more *things*.

So home life has changed. Work life has changed. What about the United States in general? That's, of course, way too big to address well here, but I can cite a recent study that ranked seventy-four countries according to their levels of stress (Bloomberg, 2013, via United Nations Office on Drugs and Crime, International Monetary Fund, Central Intelligence Agency World Factbook, Transparency International, World Health Organization)). The variables included were life expectancy, income equality, homicide rates, GDP per capita, corruption perception, urban air pollution, and unemployment. Where did the United States fall, with one being the most stressful? Fifty-four—*54!* I'll just leave it at that.

Let's recap what we've learned so far in the last two chapters: According to the women in the study, being stressed-out is a woman's plight and also a reality of living in the real world. Neither of these is likely a surprise to you, but I'm here to say neither is inevitable. We have some serious choices to make. Some big changes.

My hope is that your mind is already working on this. I hope you've been evaluating your life as you read the words of these selfless women. But we're not done yet. Next, we'll learn about the final way women talked about stress, *stressed-out as a form of social evaluation.*

More life advice from real women—Claire:

Claire: *Find time to exercise. (laughs)*

8 You Must Suffer!

***Elizabeth:** Well, Nancy and I were kind of giggling and she says, "You go to the pool?" "No, I haven't been to the pool in years," and she said, "These women that dress up, full makeup on and the jewelry and they go lay out," I said, "Does that not just kill you." And then she says when she drops off her daughter to [neighborhood] elementary, they're all just totally made up, but they have their exercise clothes on because they're getting ready to go to the gym. (**Nancy:** They're going to the gym.) And she said, "When I go to the gym, I look like I'm going to go to the gym. There's no makeup on, my hair is pulled back." I know, I mean, it's just, she says it's just this false identity.*

MEET ELIZABETH, SIXTY, AND NANCY, FIFTY. BOTH ARE MARRIED AND full-time teachers with grown children. Their conversation was actually much longer than this snippet, and you'll see the entire conversation and a deeper meaning in chapter 11. Like the other teachers you've met, they talked a great deal about the changing world of education. The new standards they have to meet. Changing student demographics. They both talked about the lovely life of retirement they had to look forward to. They had so much fun during this part of the conversation, the part about the neighborhood.

We've all done this, right? Don't lie—even if just in your own head. You've probably judged someone by her level of stress. This sort of reasoning is at the heart of why I did this study in the first place. And this stress theme is probably one you haven't thought about before, at least not on a conscious level. I had been noticing the phrases women used in response to other women's stress levels—I've mentioned some of them before:

- Wow, lucky you to have a cushy life!
- Must be nice to sleep in!
- Wish I had time to watch a movie!
- Hard day? Well welcome to my world!

Recall from chapter 1 my story of being evaluated by women in my seminar after mentioning to them I was going to have a restful weekend. This is where it all began. Sometimes we say that this kind of talk is just women being catty. You might also recall my discussion about my early impressions of these phrases: I used to call them stress competitions. I used to talk about gaining value from how stressed we were. I said women were being martyrs. In fact, here's an extract from my first book, *Life Without the Monsters*:

> **Martyrdom/Badge of Stress**
> Try to remember that the outcome of frequent outbursts of anger and self-pity is not always what we think it will be. Oftentimes we ladies wear our stressors like a badge of courage. Somehow we think people will think less of us if we admit to having time to take care of ourselves and our families.
>
> Have you ever been in a group of women (or people in general) and made a comment like, "Today I read for a while and took a little nap. I never get to do that, but I decided to allow myself an hour today to relax." Well—watch out! Many times you might hear, "Well, I wish I could do that! I don't even have time to go to the bathroom!" Usually what this means is "I choose to fill up every second of my day, allowing zero time to take care of myself. I realize that this will lead to unhappiness for me and my family. But look at me—I must be important because I'm so busy!" DO take care of yourself. Exercise, relax, and spend quality time with your family. Happy you, happy family!

> Let's stop being martyrs—at work and/or at home! The only people that suffer from this type of behavior are us! We get mad because the house isn't clean, and then we stomp around and say things like, "I'm the only one who ever does anything around here!" Then we clean up the mess and expect others to see our badge and feel terrible about what they did. We expect a parade in which we are driven down the street and recognized for our selfless act. But what really happens? No one notices. And that REALLY makes us mad! They're just glad THEY didn't have to clean up the mess.[12]

I stand by what I wrote roughly ten years ago. However, there's more to it than what I knew at the time. What I didn't consider then was the nature of women's identities. I wasn't aware of the constant societal pressure on women to be stressed-out, which leads to an evaluation of one another as we talk. This will become abundantly clear in the next few chapters as we talk about how the way we talk creates who we are. This is such a new, deep, intense way to look at stress.

Having said this, the final theme, or repertoire, I found during women's talk about stress was *stressed-out as a way of social evaluation*. This is by far the most complex repertoire of the three themes. It emerged most frequently in response to the Samantha vignette and the mattress gold-digger commercial. It also came up when women shared stories about other women not present.

This theme showed up in two ways. First, it appeared as a comparison among women with different levels of stress. You might recall Alice and Kate from earlier. I said we would evaluate Alice's words more deeply, so now it's time!

> *. . . I think, sometimes the people are like, oh, I'm not stressed-out, I'm like, well, you must not have a lot going on. (laughs) I know that sounds bad. (**Kate:** Yeah. Yeah.) (**Tami:** Well, no.) I just want you to be honest about . . . People, especially before I was pregnant, like if I said to some of my friends that have children, . . . "I haven't slept" and "I'm tired" and, "I'm stressed at work," and people will [say] "Just wait till you have kids" and that kind of thing, and it's like you're not validated if your suffering is not the same. (**Kate:** Yeah.) Yeah.*

Alice is comparing her stress levels with those of her friends. Notice a type of tagging we talked about in chapter 4. After her statement about her friends who are not stressed, she puts in *I know that sounds bad*. It could be that she was fending off any criticism from Kate and me. Or maybe she was leaving the conversation open and encouraging input. Then what happened? Not only did Kate and I *not* scold her, but we agreed with and encouraged her that she was OK. That's the rapport thing at work. So she evaluates her friends and then also points out that her friends are evaluating her. Think back to chapter 3 when I pointed out that something Alice said was the most powerful in my entire study. I'll make that point again:

It's like you're not validated if your suffering is not the same.

Kate agrees. And, they did *not* like judgment from other women! Then again, they didn't realize they were doing it. Let's look at another example of this comparison with Jacqueline. We had just finished the Posturepedic mattress commercial:

> ***Tami:*** *Tell me what you think about this "lucky" thing. People who, for example, do sleep enough, which you do, or maybe to have a low stress or don't have a lot of obligations, what you think about this whole, "Well, they must be lucky"? Have you ever said that or thought it? What do you think about that?*
>
> ***Jacqueline:*** *I think, it adds to the guilt factor. Sort of like, you know, we're lucky to get six hours of sleep, well, you must be a lazy, good for nothing gold digger, because you actually have time to get that much sleep and, meanwhile I'm trying to do this, this, this, and this and I'm a better person than you . . .*

More powerful words of wisdom from Jacqueline. On a certain level she recognizes the stress comparison among women when she notes that what might be happening is a thought of *I'm a better person than you because I have more stress*. Notice she talks about guilt here. It's a good time to point out that even though I'm writing about these themes, and soon about identities, as if they're individual necklaces in our tangled strands, they're actually all woven together. But we need to dissect them and analyze them.

One more example from Jacqueline and Grace:

Tami: *Do you think it's normal to be stressed-out?*

Jacqueline: *Yeah. I mean, everybody's stressed-out. Like, everybody has their cross to bear, you know.*

Grace: *But it does kind of bother me to hear people say that they're stressed-out when they aren't, they don't have a lot of other obligations? (**Jacqueline:** Right.)*

Tami: *Like what?*

Jacqueline: *Children.*

Grace: *Children. (laughs)*

Wow—lots of good stuff here. Everybody's stressed. In this brief interaction they tell us that everyone is stressed. Recall Samantha. So many of the ladies said that she's hiding something or the other shoe is about to drop. So, basically even someone appearing low stress has a cross to bear somewhere. Yet, if we read further, there is the comparison: some women don't have a lot of other obligations so they shouldn't be saying they're stressed. It seems the way to avoid being compared is to make sure you voice your stress. Don't hide it. If you talk about it with me, then we'll be in this club together

So Alice's comment, *It's like you're not validated if you're suffering is not the same*, is powerful. She explains that, because she does not have children, her friends do not support her when she has trouble sleeping. She is not validated. Jacqueline simply *describes* the assessment that occurs when someone actually does take time to sleep, stating that others might see her as lazy. And then Jacqueline and Grace both seem bothered when someone claims they are stressed if they don't have many obligations. So one way of talking about stress as a social evaluation is to compare our levels of stress with other women.

A second use of this theme occurred when they supported other women with similar levels of stress. Erica, like Alice, didn't have any children. She talked earlier about the expectations placed on her since she seems to have more free time. Here we're talking about her responsibilities in her department at school.

> ***Dorian:*** *Are you chairing your department?*
>
> ***Erica:*** *No, I have no interest in chairing my department.*
>
> ***Tami:*** *But you're doing all the, you're doing . . .*
>
> ***Dorian:*** *She does an inordinate amount of work with those cheerleaders. I mean, that's so time-consuming.*

When Erica says she is not interested in the responsibilities of being the chairperson of her department, Dorian quickly steps in to validate her by saying, *She does an inordinate amount of work with those cheerleaders. I mean, that's so time-consuming.* There is no judgment from Dorian that Erica has chosen not to chair her department because she's already stressed-out enough by all of her other responsibilities. She teaches *and* coaches the cheerleading team, both of which are time-consuming. There is validation here—validation that Alice says you get only if your suffering is the same. I had to wonder about the issue of similar suffering: Dorian was sixty-five and her children were grown. Would she have been as supportive of Erica if she still had children at home? Because at that time in Dorian's life, her level of suffering might have been greater than Erica's. I have no way of knowing this, but it's a thought.

Let's end by finishing up with some thoughts from Phoebe and Kay:

> ***Phoebe:*** *This is probably not very nice, but (laughs) I have a friend who, her father was really well-off when she was growing up and she married someone who's really well-off, so she doesn't have a job and she shops and does all the stuff, sleeps till, like, ten thirty every day and I just find myself being, like, I know that's not what I want to do? But I still like, wow, that'd be nice, you know?*

Kay: *But you're thinking, like, what kind of stress could she have in her [life], really?*

Phoebe: *Yeah, you're like, what would that be like? You just can't even imagine?*

What I want you to notice here as we move on to the chapters about identity, is the support. The bonding. They were nudging each other as if to say, *Yeah girl, we're in this club together!* But the friend they're describing? She's on her own. This will become so much more meaningful as we go through the next three chapters regarding women's identities. So hold on, I'm about to blow it out of the water!

More life advice from real women—Rae and Carolyn:

Rae: *My mom always says "This, too, shall pass."*

Carolyn: *Yeah, I mean, it's not going to kill you. I mean, yet. (laughs) Eventually you're probably going to have a heart attack, but I'm not going to say that to my friend. I don't know if I could say you just take one little bite at a time. And don't try to eat the whole elephant, just one little bite at a time and try to get through it.*

9

That Woman in the Mirror

Abilene: *I have two donkeys, a horse, and two dogs. We have acquired, yes, another dog since we came here. She is terrible. I happen to like down pillows. She has torn up I can't tell you how many pillows in our house, but she has torn up two feather pillows in our house, and I don't know if you've ever seen what happens when a feather pillow is opened up? And shaken by a dog, you know, yes. Two. Yesterday I came home . . . from school and there were feathers all the way down the hall and the pillow was lying in the middle of it and she had also gone into my daughter's room and taken my favorite quilt that my sister made for me out of my maternity clothes and my favorite jeans that she had cut up and made—it was such a meaningful quilt to me. Tore it to shreds. (**Bernie:** Oh no.) Shreds. You know how long it took me to clean up the feathers and, because you can't just clean them out because they fly all over creation. So I got it all in a bag and then [my husband], "What's this bag, Abilene?" I said, "Oh, that's the pillow and stuff. Needs to go out in the garbage." And you know, because I just don't even tell him anymore how pissed off I am about anything, and, because it just goes in one ear and out the other, so he left it outside the back door. Well, yesterday I came home—*

Bernie: *The dog tore it open. (laughs)*

Abilene: *YES. I had to clean the whole ding dang mess up again, two days in a row. Do you know, this is what has happened to me, though. This is my daughter, she freaks out, because when things really get crazy in my life I get very calm. And so I didn't say a word. I saw the mess on the floor, all the feathers, and I just went "[Dog's name], time to go outside." Put her on the chain, out she went, I went in and got down on my hands and knees, this is all with my ankle screwed up, the farrier on the way, and the neighbor child calls me while I'm on my knees picking up feathers to ask me if she could please come over so that I could help her with fractions. So I get very calm and I just deal with it, but let me tell you something, inside I just don't think about it. Because if I think about all the crap in my life right now, like how screwed up it is, the ironies of it, I, it makes me so mad that I just, I can't . . .*

CAN YOU IDENTIFY? EVEN IF YOU DON'T HAVE CHILDREN OR A HUSBAND, or pets, could you visualize a situation where you were selflessly giving of your time and skills and others didn't notice? Or they expected it? Or they didn't pitch in to help? So on the outside you're calm. Cool. Quiet. Maybe *scary*! What often follows an impassioned oration like this is the fact that no one appreciates what we do. No one ever helps. No one ever does what we ask. Because on the inside, we're mad. We're ticked! And when we experience a sense of resentment, it feels so real. I mean, *people should appreciate all that we do for them!* They should love us! There is a deep reason for this visceral reaction and an even deeper reason we need to fix it. It's all about who we are. It's about our identities as women.

Before moving on, let's recap the last few chapters so you'll have perspective on where we've been and where we're going. We spent chapters 5 through 8 learning ways women talk about stress. First, I opened your eyes (hopefully) to the possibility that using the word *stress* might actually take our power away because society has dictated its very meaning. Then you discovered ways women actually talk about the concept of being stressed-out. You heard women talk about it as their plight, as the reality of the world we live in today, and as a form of evaluating each other. The second goal of my study was to find out how they used those themes to tell the world who they are. In chapters 3 and 4 you learned about language. When we talk, we say to the world, T*his is a version of me.* So now it's time to see what those versions are. What kinds of identities do we create when we talk to each other, especially as it relates to stress?

At this point, you might still be thinking, *What in the world does my identity have to do with stress? I mean, the world is stressful: money, health, job, family, friends, Everything! So let's just get to it. How do I fix it?* Most stress-management books begin by telling you the world is stressful and here's how you manage it. Most will focus on the overwhelming responsibilities women have. They'll tell you to exercise, eat right, get enough sleep, let go of things, let others help you with your responsibilities, and change the way you think. These suggestions are valid—we'll actually talk about them all at some point. We absolutely should do these things. But we're not doing them. Remember, I promised you this book would be different, that I'll actually address what's keeping you from doing those things that help alleviate what the world calls stress.

We've talked about the nature of women, and I mentioned this in the introduction: If you believe that women experience stress more than men, that we're more emotional than men, that we *feel* things more than men, then you have to agree that it must have something to do with our being women. But because of cultural shifts, society today doesn't really talk about women and men as different—we talk more about how we're alike. I get it; I get the whole historical things about how women haven't exactly gotten a fair shake in many areas of life. Women haven't always been respected. This misunderstood identity is the absolute foundation of why we can't disconnect from this grueling life of stress, why we keep participating in the club.

You've heard the ladies in my study talk about expectations. Let's face it, women in the United States are still in a time and place where we are expected to play like men. When we don't, we're punished—seen as too weak to compete with the big boys. When we *do* play like men, we're punished too—called the B word. We're expected to fit into workplaces designed for men and to then adopt male values and behaviors. And many feminist researchers are still trying to discount differences between men and women, despite the abundance of research to the contrary. How did we get here? Doesn't it make sense that men and women are different? Don't we *want* some differences? We've covered this in the area of biology, but what about in the realm of psychology and, in particular, identity?

Consider this little nugget of info: Similar to the stress research we talked about in chapter 6, until the 1970s, research into how people develop a sense of identity was conducted only on men. Can you believe that? Only men; no women. Then, all that research became integrated into psychology texts, medical classes, therapy, and training, and it was taught as fact—without questioning if it applied to women. This one-sided information was eventually integrated into business books and stress-management seminars. Even today women are still being trained in assertiveness classes based on outdated models of human development. This gets me fired up!

Here's a perfect example: I was teaching a class for women about how to communicate in tough situations. It was part of a daylong women's business conference. All day I had noticed one participant and her kind, sweet spirit. During a break, several of us gathered to chat. I said to this woman, *Your suit is beautiful. You look adorable!* Her reply, consistently taught as what *not* to say in response to a compliment, was, *Oh, gosh, I don't really feel adorable! I've put on a few pounds.* Nearby, a younger woman—confident, well dressed, and articulate—spoke up. *You know what I do when a woman discounts a compliment? I pinch her! Yep. I do. And if I don't know her, like a stranger in the grocery store, I'll tell her that I'll pinch her. I say, 'I'm going to give you a compliment, and if you discount it, I'll pinch you!'* Honestly, I was thinking, *OK, if you pinch that sweet woman, I will have to punch you.* Of course, I didn't say or do this!

I'm fairly certain she had learned this technique in an assertiveness-training class she had attended. She seemed so confident that this approach would lead to the development of confidence and/or assertiveness in other women. The lesson? Punish women for behavior that, according to some theorists, is part of our nature. This nature includes the desire to maintain connectedness and to be in healthy relationships. Discounting compliments is one way that women often attempt to be relational. What I mean is, if you say I look adorable and I say *thank you,* we have basically ended the conversation and I'm now in a position above you. But if I discount it and say, *Oh, this thing—I got it at Goodwill!*, we're back on the same level and we continue to chat. This should sound familiar, as it relates to our discussion of girl talk in chapter 4.

Women have been taught that discounting a compliment or saying *sorry* are just the worst things you can do. It's problematic that some trainers teaching these classes use dated curriculum. They haven't spent time understanding the many potential reasons underlying those behaviors. Again, women are being asked to play like boys without validating and understanding their unique development.

So how does this affect us? Recall our earlier discussion about Betty Friedan and Elizabeth Pearle McKenna—about how women were living unhappy lives. Women were not happy. So what about now? In 2009, the Rockefeller Foundation, together with *Time Magazine*, published a survey that addressed the current state of gender issues. They reported gains for women in pay, education, business, and political power. Interestingly, though, they also found this: "Among the most confounding changes of all is the evidence, tracked by numerous surveys, that as women have gained more freedom, more education, and more economic power, they have become less happy."[13] *Less happy!* It wasn't the goal of the survey to address the unhappiness, but the findings are not new. Could it be that as women continue to grow in numbers in the workforce, we aren't being trained on how to exist there based on new models? Maybe it's as Jean Baker Miller put it in her 1976 book *A New Psychology of Women*: ". . . many women seriously question the values and procedures of our current institutions. The ways they are required to operate and to treat colleagues and their own families' conflict with deeply held values. Women are entering a work scene that is not likely to be totally fulfilling."[14] Miller, a psychiatrist, psychoanalyst, feminist, and author, was a social advocate for women's issues. I'll talk more about her more later.

I truly believe one reason for this unhappiness is that we might not understand who we are as women. When you look in the mirror, who is that woman staring back? It's time to think about it, consider who you are, keep what's great, and change what needs to be changed. No one teaches that. No one trains us up that we have such special, unique, and fabulous gifts as women. No one teaches that we typically thrive in healthy relationships. Nope. It's all about being independent. We don't need men. We don't need anyone. Hear us roar! Or, as it seems, it can often be more like *hear us scream for help!*

So, much of this craziness began, at least in the research, with a little man named Sigmund Freud. In 1925, Freud said this about women: *The great question that has never been answered, and which I have not yet been able to answer, despite my thirty years of research into the feminine soul, is "What does a woman want?"*

Freud was considered the pioneer in psychoanalysis. He was the authority. He wrote about things no one had considered before. The problem is, he studied only men. According to Freud, women never develop completely because we don't have penises. Go ahead and growl (or laugh). So he basically said that since men have penises, they're afraid they'll be cut off, and they'll be motivated to develop healthy identities in order to keep them. Women, due to our biological nature (i.e., no penises), should be relegated to areas that require charm, beauty, and gentleness. We will fulfill our desires for penises (I've written that word way too many times) with husbands and babies. Now don't get me wrong. I like the beauty thing—I mean, we are the beautiful gender. And I love my husband. And I loved having babies. But please—I am a person, with or without my family! Some of Freud's theories have been discounted over the years, but the effects linger, partly because he wasn't the only one saying these things.

Erik Erikson also contributed to the misunderstanding of female psychology when he developed his eight-stage life cycle. Erikson was a German-born American psychologist, probably most famous for coining the phrase *identity crisis*. He proposed that identity issues for men must be resolved before they can become intimate with another person. In other words, men must figure out who they are in the world and *then* they can have a relationship with another person. Like Freud, Erikson studied only men. Women, he said, progress differently. Because our identities are found *in* the men we choose to marry, this process might be reversed for us. In other words, we will first find intimacy with a man and *then* develop our identities. His theory is a bit more complicated than I'm making it, but the point is we were misunderstood for *so* long that it takes time to recover.

Quick personal story: On December 22, 1994, I awoke around 4 A.M. to my (then) husband saying *Wake up! The house is on fire!* It was three days before Christmas. We gathered our three children, kicked out the window screens, and escaped safely as the house burned to the ground. Since my husband was a police officer, the media was all over it, and we had newspapers and television reporters flood the house. We also had so much help from the community—it was truly amazing! So, *this* happened: A reporter from the local paper did a story on us. Here's what she said about each of us in the family:

> *What do you say to a man who is devoting his life to serving the public as a police officer then loses everything he owns in a house fire three days before Christmas?*
>
> *What do you say to his children, ages two, four, and six, when they ask where their favorite stuffed animals are?*
>
> *And what do you say to his wife who (wait for it . . .) lost every dish, pot, and pan during the most festive season of the year?*

What? *That's* what you think I was upset about? We were minutes away from dying that night! Do you know *anything* about who I am, what I do, how I think, or what's important to me? No, you do not. We could have died that night, but we all got out safely, including our dog. *That* is what was important to me. But what struck me was how she identified me: a very traditional image of a woman at home cooking, and nothing more. Now, I did perform those activities in life. But that's not *who* I was. I was a wife, mother, and healthcare worker.

I was kind, dedicated, smart . . . Anyway, you get the picture. I wasn't offended at all by her words (even though it looks like it by what I'm writing here), but it did speak volumes about how people perceive us without even knowing who we are. And we had been at a disadvantage for years in the world of research.

Back to that. Female researchers finally began to step in and research women. In 1917, Karen Horney provided one of the first of many rebuttals to these male-dominated theories when she said, *Hey, wait a minute—only the minds of men and boys are being evaluated!* In her 1932 paper T*he Dread of Woman,* she proposed that men desire materialism and domination due to the difference between *being* and *doing*. Here's what that means: Men, she said, can't get a sense of fulfillment just by being men—they have to accomplish and conquest to gain an identity. Women, she said, fulfill themselves by the very nature of *being*; a woman, regardless of lifestyle choice, has the ability to bear a child. There is no need to *do* anything to feel value. We have the ability to create life! Men, on the other hand, lack this gift and so must fulfill themselves by *doing*. This is a beautiful description of the female identity. Think of how different the lives of women would be if society valued us this way. I realize there will be women reading this who choose not to have children or can't have children, but that's not the issue here. It's a matter of a deep subconscious feeling of worth based on the fact that our gender has been entrusted to continue life on this planet.

So, do men not need relationships at all? Are they only task-oriented? Jean Baker Miller writes that *all* development, even men, occurs within relationships. But men are typically raised to be independent. And the old theories by guys such as Freud and Erikson insisted upon separation. This separation has led to the development of a hierarchy, and the gender demonstrating the behaviors valued by society become dominant.

What does this mean? Society tends to value independence, assertiveness, goals, and accomplishments. And we tend to associate these traits with men. So who becomes the dominant gender? Men. Women, then, are devalued as the inferior gender, and we might look at male behaviors as those that are more desirable. I don't mean for this to sound like a male-bashing book, because it's absolutely not. I just feel bad for us as women, feeling like we often have to squelch our natures. And I also feel bad for men who often have to do the same. Unfortunately, there's not much research out there about men developing their identities within healthy relationships, but through the years there has been quite a lot for women.

Miller wrote her book to make one colossal point: In order to survive as a society, people must serve the needs of one another. The problem in our society is that this service is not valued. Women might be better suited to recognizing and responding to the needs of others. In fact, Miller proposes we thrive in this context. *Unless* we are forced to. When this happens, the individual needs of the mother/wife/worker are left unmet. Opportunities to integrate service with personal growth are limited. So women are left with the internal conflict of having to choose between serving *either* others *or* ourselves. This leaves women gaining power but feeling empty.

Understand that relationships are not just marriage and parenting, although those might be part of yours. They are far more than that. Being in healthy relationships means having good friends, relating well to coworkers, and having or being a relational boss—those types of relationships. For *all* humans, Miller says five good things come from these mutually empathic, growth-promoting relationships: the empowerment to act, vitality, self-worth, the desire to have more connection, and greater knowledge of self and others. Love this!

Other female psychologists have written about the multiple dimensions of the female identity. Nancy Chodorow (1978) wrote about developing identities within the mother/daughter relationship. Another of my female psychology heroines is Ruthellen Josselson. She describes women, work, and identity this way.[15] "Too often, researchers and writers make a sharp distinction between woman as worker—productive employee or creator—and woman as relator to others, as though there were indeed two quite separate aspects of a woman that are inevitably in conflict." My goodness, isn't that so true. Although we might have a particular identity at work, most women do not shut off their relational selves just because they sit down at that desk (or whatever the workplace might be for them).

I have a fun personality quiz I created a few years ago (See www.tamiwest.com). We take it together in some of my seminars, and inevitably someone will raise her hand and ask, *Do I answer this as I am at work or at home?* I get that we have many different types of behaviors during our days, but I think we really do see ourselves as having multiple personalities! Even if you don't have a job outside the home, you can relate this to other parts of your life. This is the issue with today's workplace training for women, relationships only get mentioned as opposed to included. There is no mention of the relationship risks of saying no, and no attempts are made to work through the internal conflicts we have as women in so many roles. In these classes, conversations with women consistently reveal deep confusion about identities. And the women in my study showed equal confusion. You've already met Sondra. *Feel* the struggle in her words:

> *I would say expectations to me are huge. And it comes from all sorts of areas, you know? Like making sure the corporate office is happy, making sure the employees are happy, and just settling all the things that come up throughout the day, which are many every day. Making sure that everything's taken care of, everybody's taken care of, making sure I'm doing everything that I'm supposed to do with outside responsibilities in the community, like Rotary or coalition groups or boards that I'm on and then church. It's like I want to do it all, I want to be 110 percent in everything (**Tami:** Everything.) Everything. And I want to give 110 percent and I want to be 110 percent. And then when you do have a family situation like Grandmother had surgery recently and was very ill and I just was really concerned whether or not she was going to make it, you know, you add that to everything else . . .*

Have you ever been in Sondra's shoes? *I just want everyone to be happy. I just want to do a good job. I want my family to be cared for. I want to do it all. And then, if something unexpected comes up—then what?*

Sondra exemplifies many women in this world. Through it all, notice her desire to be connected. She wants everyone taken care of.

She wants people in her world to be happy. She wants to be there for her family. Of course, Sondra certainly has business and financial goals she wants to achieve, but this entire conversation centered on relationships. What you can't see in her words is her heartfelt tone. Her furrowed brow. Her expressive eyes and hand movements. Her passion for her job, family, and community. Sondra, like all of us, lives in a world that doesn't fully understand and embrace our varied identities as women.

Back to my earlier assumption that it might be hard to grasp the connection between identity and stress. I've used the word *identity* many times. At this point, you probably need a definition, so let's use one from the Internet (www.yourdictionary.com). We'll base our entire discussion about identity on this very generic definition (I trimmed it a little):

> *The definition of identity is who you are, the way you think about yourself, and the way you are viewed by the world.*

There are three parts to this generic definition:

- Who are you?
- How do you think about yourself?
- How does the world view you?

Based on this, then, let's look again at Abilene's words opening this chapter. How could we describe her identity? My identity? Your identity?

When you think about the first question, *Who are you?* from this definition, it can seem on the one hand very concrete, very factual. On the other hand it can go deep! For our purposes, we'll describe this part of your identity as the part that isn't dependent on what you think or what others think about you. These parts of your identity are often obvious, so this one is actually pretty easy: Abilene is a woman, a mom, a daughter, a sister, a teacher, a neighbor, and a pet owner. Biologically, she is defined by her ovaries—her ability to bear children. (Remember, I don't mean we're all just baby-making machines.) And that influences other identities we have such as wife and mother. We have a uterus, ovaries, and hormones.

So that's what we know about Abilene. What about me? I am a woman, wife, mother, speaker, and author. Oh, don't worry, we are definitely coming back to *you* in chapter 12, where we will work on your exit strategy.

The second question, *How do you think about yourself?* gets a little more complicated. This one isn't necessarily factual; it can be influenced by our biology, *is* dependent on what we think, and certainly can be influenced by what others think of us. We carry around thoughts, or models, about ourselves and often don't even realize it. We are then shaped by these models. Sometimes we label these models according to how we *feel*. For Abilene, it appears she thinks/feels she is tired, *pissed*, *annoyed*, busy, overwhelmed, stressed, at her wits end, taken advantage of—we could go on. Notice that these aren't really feelings, they're thoughts. But they are descriptive words, they're subjective, and they can and do change.

I recently searched the phrase *your true identity* on Amazon and got 965 results. Searching *identity* yielded 2,790, and *Who am I?* generated the most with 350,866 results. When we're searching for help with our identities, what we're often looking for is how we think about ourselves. I'm sure since the dawn of time humans have asked questions like this. But when you read the descriptions of these books, they seem to fall into two categories. One type of identity book is really more of an instructional book. A particular book description tells readers they will d*iscover the incredible power they have over their experience of life, finding the doorway to eternal peace, happiness, and fulfillment.* So it really seems to be teaching what I should *do*. That's not a bad thing, but it still doesn't tell me who I *am*.

A second group of books are really descriptors of a particular identity, like *Who Am I? Identity in Christ.* As a Christian woman I value this type of book. It can be helpful in discovering who I am. But I'm not so sure it helps the Christian woman as much as it does the Christian man. These kind of books are written by people with their own thoughts, experiences, and opinions, and, as such, are interpretations. Sometimes those interpretations, often written by men, can be damaging for women.

So what about me? Who do I *think* I am? I think I'm happy (usually), complicated, smart (sometimes), driven (or so I've been told), moody (aren't we all?)—we could go on here, too!

I want to point out something interesting that happened as I wrote about myself. Notice what I did—I put "disclaimers" after each of my positive statements, the statements that might make you believe I was a little full of myself, with words such as *smart* and *happy*. As discussed in chapter 4, we're often told that we add on these little tags because we aren't confident. Same thing with apologies. In other words, I say I'm smart, but then I kind of take it back. I say that I'm driven, but then I hedge a bit. Remember the pinch story—same thing! While it might be true that I do that because I'm not confident, there's that other issue of being relational.

The third question, *How does the world view me?* has a couple of connotations and is really at the heart of what differentiates my approach to stress. First, *the world* can be taken to mean society in general. It only takes watching television—sitcoms, commercials, etc.—to figure out what society thinks of us and who we are. In the fifties, sixties, seventies, and today, we can see definite stereotypes of women.

Think about your mother or your grandmother or your great-grandmother—depending on how old you are. Who were women in the fifties and sixties? Well (if they were *good* women, at least), they were spouses, mothers, volunteers, friends, obedient daughters, and sisters. They were *not* career-minded, political, smart, or contributors to society in general. And then came the seventies—the *I can do it all woman*! That rolled into the eighties, which brought along the *Enjoli* woman. Depending on your age, you may recall this perfume commercial depicting the modern eighties woman wearing this empowering perfume, bringing home the bacon, frying it up in a pan, and never forgetting her man. Fast forward a few years to 2015 with Sheryl Sandburg's book *Lean In*. Not only *can* you do it all, but you *should*. Get in that boardroom! Lean in to that conversation! Be heard! Climb the ladder! You can do it! I actually respect Sheryl, all she's done, and quite a bit of what she's written. But, again, it sets a tone for who women should be.

A second meaning of the *world* is those you interact with—mother, sister, friends, daughter, coworkers, etc. Unlike the broad messages we get from society in general, our closer world often tells us to our faces what they think of us, right?! Maybe you heard through the grapevine that your friends think you've put on a few pounds. ☹ Or maybe you just got a promotion at work and you get the cold shoulder from your coworkers turned employees; you heard they've been saying you're *full of yourself*. These are often people who matter to us, the ones with whom we have relationships. How these humans think about us contributes to our identities. It shapes our thoughts about ourselves.

All three components of your identity are important. There are certain parts of you that are simply who you are, certain parts you think into being, and certain parts created when you interact with others. You've met Abilene a time or two. Here, she tells us how special and sweet it is to just be ourselves:

> ***Abilene:*** *(laughs) Oh, my God, I love women. See, my best friend's husband died over the fall break and as soon as I knew that he was gone, I booked a flight and was out of here. And spent a lot of the break up there with her, . . . my daughter and her daughter are dearest best friends and she's my best friend. And so we went up there and, . . . of course my . . . my daughter converged and I converged and the four of us or as soon as everybody else was sort of gone, we had a girls' night like we used to always have back home. I love girls' nights, it was so awesome and I miss them so bad, because you just get to be, you know any time a woman really gets to be herself is when she's with the girls, like that's it. Like, that's it. And so . . . we were able to just let it go and just do whatever we were doing, like "Gangnam" [popular song from South Korean musician PSY] dance in the kitchen. Like, that is awesome. Right? I mean, and here's, her husband just died but we're all dancing in the kitchen to this song, you know what I mean, but it was just such a release, it was so great to just be able to just be ourselves, because that's the only time . . .*

I love this story! Even amidst a tragedy such as death, women, in positive relationships, can help each other be who we want to be! Compare this to the earlier pinching story. When I'm with my girlfriends and I have the opportunity to help or guide someone, I sometimes ask myself, *pinch or dance*? I try to pick dance. I want to support and encourage as much as possible. Judging and criticizing can be someone else's thing.

You're ready now to see the next two chapters and the identities women created during their conversations about stress: *I'm a responsible woman* and *I'm like you.* I'll leave this chapter with some quotes to ponder. Before writing this book, I posted a call for help on Facebook: *Help: I'd like input for my upcoming book. In one sentence, what would you say I need to include regarding women and stress? I'd love for you to leave that comment here!* Here you go—enjoy, relate, think, and consider how much identity connects with what these women had to say:

- *All women are different . . . some can handle being a full-time, working, do-it-all mom. Other women who do not work, still have stress! Depends on the family structure in my opinion. BTW . . . I work full-time, take care of the house and laundry . . . no help from the men in my house. Tried tough love . . . has worked some . . . but not much . . . sometimes I just would like to run away . . .*
- *We are too blessed to be stressed. Trust in the Lord entirely and look to him for guidance every day.*
- *I tend to thrive, or at least I think I do, when I have eight things going on at once, but often fail to consider how my too-full-plate affects my husband and daughter. I think how our stress affects others is important.*
- *Peace and be still.*
- *Stress takes away joy.*
- *One definition of stress is to be pulled in all directions. As women we try to do everything. Making us feel stressed. Sometimes just taking a moment to figure out what our true priorities are can*

help. Also letting go of the not-so-important things. Life is too short. At the end of the day, if it doesn't hurt someone maybe it's just not a priority.

- *I think external cultural pressure needs to be addressed especially in the context of "traditional gender roles" and expectations.*
- *Just pray about it.*
- *Physical manifestations of stress in our bodies. Not just health but the way our bodies behave under stress. Fatigue, weight gain, aches and pains. Also stress as a major trigger for depression.*
- *Stressed is just desserts spelled backwards!*
- *We take on too much. Emotionally, financially. Personally. I've found that Let Go and Let God works for me. Too much is not good for us. One breath at a time.*
- *Laughter.*
- *Stress steals peace.*
- *We need to understand we were born perfectly imperfect. Being a perfectionist is something we will never be! Trying to be the impossible will cause stress for sure.*
- *You cannot pour from an empty cup, so it is imperative that you care for yourself.*
- *The tendency to overthink in stressful situations.*
- *My family's expectations sometimes bury me.*
- *If it isn't going to change your life dramatically, let it go, and pick your battles, don't let them pick you.*
- *CORTISOL. This word was not in my vocabulary. What I didn't know is that if your cortisol levels are maxed out your entire body reacts with fatigue, weight gain and a host of other issues. So instead of being able to manage stress I am now taking a PILL or two or three to deal with the effects of a high cortisol*

level. Reflecting, change your attitude and make daily tasks wants rather than have to. Sounds silly and takes self-reminding but it works. Every little relief adds up. Yes, easier to say than do but when I lay in bed at night I tend to feel better about my day. PS. Your age and where you are in your life has so much to do with it. One thing I wish I had been better prepared for in life is more education pre-menopause so I would have been able to prepare rather than react because these decisions will be detrimental to your day-to-day quality of life.

o *Do an agenda/things to do and make yourself number 1. Always find some time for you.*

o *That God is our only source during times of trouble because when we look to man, he can fail us but God never will in any circumstance or situation.*

o *Why is it in any given day I can remember a hundred different details as long as I forget one. I know this so as long as I can figure out what that one thing was that I forgot—then I feel somewhat satisfied about my productivity.*

o *We need to learn to go easy on ourselves. To not try to live up to some "Supermom/woman" ideal. To go easy on each other. We need to show other women the grace we so long for. We also need to not be ashamed to take a break, to be "lazy" from time to time. We should be able to be happy and not think we have to fit into some stereotype that all women are stressed and have to have everything all together all the time.*

o *In addition to the above, nutrition plays an important role—getting enough fruits and vegetables to help reduce oxidative stress, which damages artery walls and cells, in general, is key.*

o *How damaging stress can be to overall physical health.*

o *Women tend to carry the weight of the world on their shoulders, worrying about family, friends, work, to-do lists . . . we need to find a healthy way to stand up straight and manage the weight-bearing stress.*

- *Women need to learn not to stress themselves out with the little things in life. You can only do what you can do in a day, save the rest for tomorrow!*

More life advice from real women—Kay and Phoebe:

Kay: *If it were me I would tell her just to take one piece at a time, and instead of looking at it as a whole deal take one aspect at a time and break it down. And, of course, the first thing we do, I just pray about it and, just pray for God to prioritize what needs to be done and what can be taken out . . .*

Kay: *So this is why I started leaving at four o'clock every day (laughs), because that was one of those things I said, six, seven o'clock, supper wasn't getting done. It was the kids' bedtime, [son] was in kindergarten, so I can't live like this. I'm missing the time that I have, so that that's when I started leaving at four. (laughs)*

Phoebe: *I would definitely say pray about it, too, and I feel like you'll just get what you need after that and prioritize. I had something just a minute ago, but I lost it. (laughs)*

Kay: *Because of all that stuff up there. You're sitting here trying to find out what you've got to do next. (laughs)*

Phoebe: *I can't remember.*

Kay: *Good at that. (laughs)*

Push, Push, Push, Push

Lydia: *I would love six hours of sleep.*

Tami: *(laughs) You would love six hours of sleep. (**Lydia:** Mm-hmm.) Okay.*

Dalia: *I try not to go to sleep during the day. I am to that point where I now drink caffeine. If I had no responsibilities like that [Judith Goldrush, gold digger], I would be crazy because I had no responsibilities. I would be looking for responsibilities. I would be looking for those things that cause me stress anyway. Because I have to have something to do. And it has to be something meaningful; it can't be something that has no meaning.*

LET'S FOCUS SOME ON WOMEN AS BUSY PEOPLE. WE'RE BUSY, RIGHT? We have responsibilities, right? It keeps us from sleeping, right? Or . . . does it?

For the ten years I taught high school, I had children at home. During the school year, I was *busy*! I would get up in the morning, get myself ready, and then get the children ready (to include showers, lunches, last-minute signatures, and those checks that have to be written to every teacher for every imaginable fee.). I would drop off the kids at their schools, and then rush to get to my school on time. I was busy all day at school. At the end of my workday I would leave school, pick up the kids, take them to their sports, prepare dinner, do my own homework, bedtime, and then get up the next day and do it all again.

And then . . . summertime came.

As the kids got older and were able to do more things for themselves, I became less busy. When my husband came home at the end of his workday and asked me how my day was, I *certainly* wasn't going to say it was relaxing! *Are you kidding me?* I wouldn't say that I watched the hummingbirds for a while, read a little, ran a few errands, talked to my mom, cleaned up a little, and spent time with the kids. No. The conversation focused on what I *had* to do: *Well! I had to clean the house, deal with the kids' fighting, listen to my mom drive me nuts, and run a million errands.*

It wasn't until I was engaged in my study that I began to reflect on why I had made that choice to *not* discuss a pleasant day with my husband. If I had described that relaxing day to my husband (or to anyone actually), what might he had thought of me? Would he have thought I was lazy? Maybe he would have thought my life was easy while his stressful life went on at work. He might even have said something like, *Wow, I wish I had your life!* During my time of reflection, I realized that's a risk I wasn't ready to take. I wanted to be seen in a certain way. I still unknowingly wanted—I'll even say needed—to be in the club. During the school year, I identified myself as busy, productive, and interesting—the same as other women. During the summer, though, *who was I?* I had no identity that I could see. I wasn't productive; I wasn't busy; I didn't see myself as interesting; and I was set apart from those other women whose regular jobs kept them busy during most of the summer (the part where they weren't taking vacations).

On top of all that, even with my summers free from fulltime work, I completely refused to enjoy the summers as the kids got older. Yes, looking back, it was a refusal. But . . . during their younger years, I *did* enjoy summer! Why was that? It was because when the children were younger, I was still super busy during the summers doing the things that moms do. Stay-at-home moms are certainly not given the credit they deserve for that identity! Taking care of my young children all summer allowed me to fulfill my busy identity during those months. It would be something like, *I am doing all that I can for my family. I am responsible, productive, and a good mother.* So it had to do with how I identified myself.

Something else interesting happened when school started each year. I had a wonderful principal—he truly was a kind man. BUT . . . each year when we had our big, back-to-school teacher meeting, he would have the same speech. It went something like this:

> *I want to welcome back the best teachers in the county. Now that school is beginning, I know you'll be here before the sun comes up! And you'll be here well after the doors close! I know you take work home and put your whole selves into this job. And for that, I applaud you!*

And then he would clap. Everyone would then clap. Like we discussed before, there would be nudging and laughing. *What?* . . . What? So is that what we're *supposed* to do? What if I don't want to be here before the sun rises? What if I'd like to be home with my family not long after the doors close? What if I finish my work and don't bring stuff home? Does that make me irresponsible? Oh my, what to do?

We talked in chapter 5 about media messages and the researchers who looked at advertisements in women's magazines. I actually perused a few myself, as well as other messages out there. Here are a few:

- One ad is for mini blinds. It shows a woman leaning on a window saying, *I go a million miles an hour, so I conserve energy everywhere else I can.*
- Another ad for makeup has a very peaceful-looking woman saying this: *We all have to do ten things at once. Perfectly.*
- On a rental car shuttle bus, I saw a sign that said, *Like you've got time for a receipt.*
- A final one is a television commercial for a car. The voiceover says, *You. We know you. We know you have to rise early and work late. With not enough sleep in between.*

Hmm. Consider this:

What if you don't want to run a million miles an hour? What if doing ten things at once perfectly has caused you a great deal of unhappiness? What if you do have time for a receipt? And, that voice doesn't know you! He's not your Facebook friend. He doesn't come to your kids' parties. He doesn't send you birthday cards nor would he recognize you in the mall. But he knows you?

I don't think so! He knows who society *says* you are!

What are the underlying messages: *life is supposed to be busy, crazy, unhappy, and stressed!* So what happens then? Well, if you're not busy, crazy, unhappy, and stressed, then something's wrong with you. Maybe you're not responsible! You're for sure not in the club. A big issue for women's identities is the belief systems we've developed over lifetimes of experiences between us and the world. These messages feed into who we are and the identities we create when we talk.

It might be helpful here to throw in a reminder of what I mean by *identities we create when we talk*. Let's say that you're married with three small children, and your husband just got out of the hospital. You work full time, and now you have to do your job, take care of the kids, *and* care for your recuperating husband. One day you and I are talking, and you mention that you have to pick up your husband's medicine from the pharmacy after work, get dinner going, help kids with homework, and then work on a project. I say to you, I'll pick up the medicine, get the kids, and pick up something for dinner. You just go home and take care of your sick husband and get your work done. I'm great, huh? So later when you talk about me (and you *will* talk about me!), what will you say? Most likely you will say how nice or kind or sweet I am, or something like that. That's an identity. Notice I didn't *tell* you I was nice or kind or sweet—but the words I used said it for me. It's the same thing with how we talk about stress. We're telling other people, *Hey, this is a version of me*—at least in this current conversation.

After I determined the most common themes (interpretative repertoires) these women used (chapters 6–8), I wanted to know how they used those themes to position themselves in the conversation, or to create their identities. Remember, we are joining in with voices of past and present—other women who are and have been talking about stress. There are word choices to make; depending on the situation, some are safer than others.

The first identity that most of the women in my study created was, *I am a responsible woman.* This identity emerged often when they chatted about the lack of self-care and also when they talked about their stressors. They used words such as *perfectionist, OCD, guilt, worry*, etc., as they described their daily obligations. They were *really* vocal about being responsible after watching the mattress commercial. They would watch, and then I would ask them about the real world, sleep, and self-care. I found three ways that they used the themes to create the responsible identity. One way was to choose from the *real world* theme and talk about their days using terms such as *whirlwind, rushing,* and *crazy*. Read as Rae describes her busy days:

> *Twenty years. I've been a coach twenty years. I have some helpers, but they're in college, so this semester I've had only [little time with them]. They could come at five o'clock or they maybe could come on a Saturday or Sunday, so I've really been on my own, kind of, is how to look at it. And from the minute I get up I'm on my feet just running, washing clothes while cooking breakfast and then trying to get the kids down and then rushing to school when they're at different schools, so doing the drop-off and making sure everybody has their lunch and, "Oh my gosh, I forgot to give you the water for break time," and (laughs) then getting to school and it's just on! It just seems like push, push, push, push, and you don't have time to sit. I mean, I eat my breakfast, I'm holding my bowl while I'm cooking bacon on the stove, and my kids, I fix breakfast, that was something my mom taught me. I don't do just a quick cereal thing. I always cook something and I have practice as soon as I get out of class. It starts at three thirty, so I straighten my desk, I go for my backpack, and I go straight to practice and stay till five thirty, six-ish? Then drive home,*

figure out who needs to be driven to [location] for dance. Is there a ball game that night? Who has to be at the backgame? And it's just, it's a whirlwind, and then it gets ten o'clock and it's time to grade papers. And the kids want to know, "did you grade those papers last night?" (laughs).

Rae was creating for herself an identity as a responsible woman by taking us through her day. She talks about going above and beyond the call of duty. She is on her feet running from the minute she gets up. She seems frustrated when she says, *and it's just on, it just seems like push, push, push, push, and you don't have time to sit.* She speaks about her mom teaching her to cook something as opposed to doing a cereal thing, drawing on the woman's plight theme. She's a good mother.

As I talked with Rae and later listened to the audio, I thought so much about the story I shared with you earlier. Those are exactly the words I would use—*every single time I talked. No matter what the day was really like!* I'm not saying Rae didn't do all of those things, but for all of us women I have to believe there are *some* days that aren't quite so crazy. There were for me, but I *always* needed to be responsible. I just couldn't stand the thought that I might appear lazy!

A second way the women created themselves as responsible was to describe a positive self-care choice they made followed by a disclaimer of responsibility. Let's hear again from Erica and then Ginger—they're actually two separate conversations:

Tami: *So, let me ask first, do you feel like it's important to take care of yourself?*

Erica: *I mean, I'll be honest, no one's told me that I can or can't, but because I don't get out of here . . . I take myself downstairs and work out during my planning periods. You know what, at the end of the day, I'm OCD, I'm a perfectionist. My work, I swear to you, is in [by] end of the day it's assigned, like, kids turn something in and it doesn't matter what time [they turn it in], it's going to get turned in [grades posted online], it may not be until tonight when I get home? So, for* *that sake, because I know at six o'clock that's not the time when I can go work out, I'm exhausted. So, I take my happy self down there and do it during the day and, honest to goodness, I dare somebody to say anything. Because everybody knows my work is in. Everybody knows I don't have a normal schedule . . .*

Tami: *So, do you get enough sleep on a regular, fairly regular basis?*

Ginger: *I do. I have to have my sleep and I know that about myself. There is a point that when I am up too long, it's crazy, but I know my body, but there's a point when my stomach starts hurting and I start feeling ill and if I don't go to sleep, I'm going to be a wreck pretty quick. It happens pretty quick, so I do get enough sleep. That's a huge priority in my life, but I'm not lazy. I mean, I'm up by 4:45. Well it's not that I sleep [too much] . . . and I don't take naps and I don't sleep on the weekend and stuff, so . . .*

Here, Erica admits that she *does* take time to exercise. But think about all we've learned so far: What if Erica had stopped earlier in her conversation? You know, just said, *Hey, yeah, I do exercise and take care of myself!* The risk? Another woman in that conversation might have said, *Phew, must be nice!* Out of the club goes Erica. How to avoid that risk? Follow it with a disclaimer. So Erica follows up with perfectionism and OCD, explaining that her work is done every day and *everybody knows my work is in. Everybody knows I don't have a normal schedule.* In other words, *I'm responsible so don't even TRY to say I'm not!* Ginger admits to getting enough sleep and then quickly follows up with the fact that she is not lazy, gets up at 4:45, and does not nap or sleep on the weekends. Again, same risk if she simply says she sleeps, she's out of the club.

Notice what themes they used to create themselves as responsible here: the *real world* and the *social evaluation* themes.

Let me point out something else. These conversations are also excellent representations of something about which I told you in chapter 3—ideological dilemmas. Recall we talked about the struggle that goes on about what identity to adopt. You can tell here that both Erica and Ginger seem to recognize the importance of self-care, but neither admit, without a disclaimer, to doing it. So, even though I can't know what they're thinking, it appears that they are struggling with knowing that an identity of self-care is ideal, but having one can be risky and leave them alone & feeling judged!

A final way responsibility was created came when they compared themselves to someone else who apparently lacked responsibility. Dalia and Lydia were talking about Judith Goldrush—they're just not buying it:

> ***Dalia:*** *I think they are hiding something. (laughs)*
>
> ***Tami:*** *(laughs) You think they're hiding something.*
>
> ***Dalia:*** *I do. I don't think that that's realistic. I think the cushy life comes with a price. So . . .*
>
> ***Tami:*** *What's the price? And what's the cushy life?*
>
> ***Dalia:*** *Well, the picture of her, the picture with that woman and her husband? He's elderly. Now, does she really love him? Is her love life okay? Is her emotional connection to her husband okay? Is that the kind of life she really wanted?*
>
> ***Lydia:*** *I think when they say lucky, I don't know. To me she was not a responsible person. (**Dalia:** Mm-hmm.) Because in real life, we have responsibilities, and those responsibilities are sometimes what cuts into the sleep. Like when I went to school and I was working and my husband worked second shift, they [children] came first. Their homework came first. Their laundry did and their supper and their basketball and their piano practice, so when they went to bed at ten, well, that's when I did my work. My school work. So I think sometimes when you see commercials like that, I don't relate to them, because I'm like, well, what responsibilities does this lady have?*
>
> ***Dalia:*** *Well, and it looks narcissistic. She looks very narcissistic.*

*Her life is all about her. If she doesn't have any responsibilities, honest-to-goodness, is she really happy? Because I . . . we got into teaching, not because we thought, Oh, we want to, we want our summers off (because that doesn't happen), and we want to pay for education that we're going to get very little in return for and we want to teach kids all day long. You know, [it] has its own challenges and we want to teach special kids and there has to be a purpose to happiness. (**Tami:** That's interesting.) And how can you have a purpose, and. . . I think in general, that's my opinion.*

Dalia and Lydia were very clear on their responsibilities in the world and the importance of fulfilling those duties. As with most of the other conversational partners, they questioned the authenticity of the mattress commercial actress, assuming that she's hiding something and most certainly unhappy. Then they both labeled her as irresponsible and narcissistic. Lydia pointed out that sometimes responsibilities in life cut into sleep. She then described her life with school, a husband, and children, and how she prioritizes those duties. Dalia told us that there must be a *purpose to happiness*, equating this happiness to responsibility. She then described her purpose as being to teach special children.

Even before I conducted the study, I had seen this issue of responsibility surface on a number of occasions. In November 2014 I did a series of webinars titled "A Gathering of Women." (If you were a participant—hello again and thank you.) During the first session, I had the attendees read an article from *Working Mother* magazine (October 2010). In the article, author Marlene Arute describes her *Me* day gone bad. You'll find a transcript in chapter 12 when you create your exit strategy. For months, as Marlene writes it, she had been trying to take some time to get a manicure, see a movie, or go shopping. I asked the women on the call to tell me what they thought of this woman who just wanted some *me time*. They wrote:

stressed, busy, selfish, ridiculous thinking she should have time for herself, lazy, high strung, busy, stressed, at her breaking point

Then I said, ‘Let’s do a virtual hand raise. How many of you can identify with her—even if not a mom—about how your time goes? If you feel like your life is craziness! Hand raise. OK, 70 percent. Wow!” Others just wrote in *stressed*, *selfish*, and *dishonest*. Many of them did not like that this woman wanted a day to herself and then grumbled when it didn’t happen. How dare we think it’s acceptable not to participate in *club* activities, aka craziness. By this point in the book, I hope you are rethinking this approach to life. I hope you’re realizing the power of voluntary activities: Now that your eyes have been opened to your inclusion in this club, you can plan a strategy to get out!

Finally, a couple of recent experiences with this identity I want to share with you. First, I recently attended the School Nutrition Association’s national conference. The majority of the members of this association are those who work in school food service. Mostly women, these *lunch ladies*, as they’re often called, work tirelessly to serve our nation’s children. I’ve met thousands of them when I speak at conferences, and 99 percent are kind, hardworking, caring, and loads of fun! Most don’t get the respect they deserve. When they go to these conferences, they like to kick back, have fun, and bond with each other. This badge seen on the previous page was a type of bonding that makes me cringe.

If you've been to events like that, you might have seen or even worn badges with ribbons on them (see photo on opposite page). What do I think about this one?

NO! NO! NO! NO! NO!

Please never identify yourself this way! *Workaholic* and *OCD* are not synonymous with *responsible.* They are identities that are damaging and restrictive. They are the pots of water, leading us to feel like addictions and obsessions are normal. I realize these labels lead to a bonding among professionals, but it's not the type of bonding that's healthy.

Second, Facebook. Take a look at this conversation among women (of course, names have been hidden):

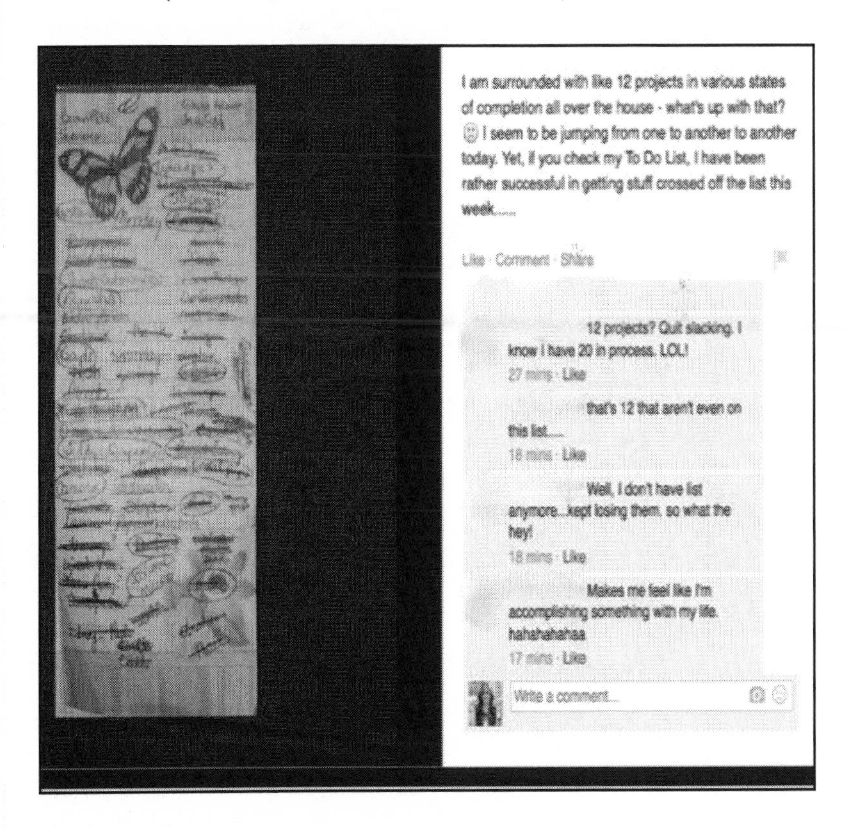

What do I think about this one?

NO! NO! NO! NO! NO!

Try hard to refrain from posting about your busyness. Don't strive to be in the Stress Club. Be careful about competitions like you see here because *there* will be a winner, and I don't want it to be you. And definitely don't attempt to become president of the club!

These are the exact types of identity creations we've been talking about in this chapter. Protect your identity! Make a decision about who you want to be. Don't let the world tell you that you must be constantly busy, crazy, OCD, or a perfectionist. These characteristics are not equated with responsibility. *You* decide what responsibility means to you. And then live accordingly.

Well, lots of words. Lots of struggles. Lots of sleeplessness and busy lives. So is it OK to be busy? I believe we were created to be productive, to have a purpose, and to live fulfilling lives. But I hope you saw the issue here, another hidden issue that keeps us from disconnecting from stress. The risk of self-care, down time, exercise, and sleep is being seen as irresponsible. Which is not true! We are *supposed* to take care of our bodies. We *need* sleep and downtime. I hope you're continuing to self-assess and preparing yourself for your strategy, Now onto the next identity: *I'm like you!*

More life advice from real women—Ginger and Candy:

Ginger: *[If I were talking to a stressed-out friend], I would introduce her to Christ, if she didn't know. If she didn't, if she wasn't a believer, then I would tell her that I was not really sure how she did it apart from that and that this is how I do it. This is what I do, prayer is a big part of my life and I do pray throughout the day. I always start my day—excuse me, I try to start my day by talking with the Lord and by having a conversation with him and leaning on h.*

Candy: *Yeah, I'm probably not quite as open as Ginger, but I probably find out first if they're a Christian or not, you know, where they're at in their life. Because if they're Christian, of* *course what I'm going to tell them is to start praying—get in the Word so that you can have that Living Word and that's going to be the one thing that gets you where you need to be, because God's going to put you in that place. But if they're not, I've never thought about approaching it that way. It's a great way to approach it, is just to be a witness like, I don't know how you do it. (laughs) This is how I help to manage my stress and, I'd probably just talk to them also about. . . what do they have going on in their life that they can take off their plate, you know? There are things that you can give to someone else to do and that kind of [thing].*

Tami: *Changes they can make?*

Candy: *Yeah. Yeah. And then just make myself available to talk to them.*

Ginger: *And a good massage never hurts, but (laughs) it's only temporary, I mean, really.*

Candy: *Yeah.*

Dressed to the Nines

Tami: *So, tell me, did you have a chance to look at it [the Relaxity ad]? Okay. So tell me about this woman on the left* [the woman without Relaxity].

Roxy: *(laughs) That's what I feel like* (woman on left), *but that's what I act like* (woman on right). *My phrase is "fake it till you make it."*

Mishae: *I love that. She told me that like a year, year and a half ago.*

Roxy: *Yes. That's going to be, if I write a book, that's going to be the title.*

Tami: *If you describe the woman on the left, like the . . .*

Roxy: *And that's often what I try to present.*

Tami: *Which is what? Like, describe, tell me about the woman on the left.*

Mishea: *Frazzled.*

Roxy: *Frazzled, yeah.*

Mishae: *Disgruntled.*

Tami: *Okay.*

Mishae: *Ugh.*

Roxy: *Not really dis-, I mean, just . . .*

Mishae: *She dropped her coffee? That's me.*

Roxy: *Rushing? Yeah. (laughs)*

Tami: *That's true, you did spill it on you before you got here.*

Mishae: *Exactly. (laughs)*

Tami: *Describe the woman on the right [same woman after Relaxity].*

Roxy: *She's got it all together. (**Tami:** Right.) Everything's going great. She's she's skinny. (**Tami:** She's skinny?)*

Mishae: *She didn't drop her coffee. (**Tami:** She didn't drop her coffee.)*

Roxy: *Yeah, she looks relaxed, calm, she's standing upright, her body language is just speaking "I'm comfortable, things are going good for me," probably going to the mall, you know (laughs), "I don't have to work today because I don't have to ever work."*

Mishae: *"Because my doctor husband's taking care of me."*

Roxy: *Yes. "And he's the one who's stressed on Relaxity and I'm not, you know, I'm just . . ." (laughs)*

Tami: *You got her all figured out.*

Roxy: *Yes. Shops at Whole Foods. And she's got healthy groceries, you know, eating expensive stuff.*

Tami: *She does have some fruits and vegetables there, doesn't she?*

Roxy: *She does. Whole Foods.*

Mishae: *Mm-hmm.*

ROXY AND MISHAE ARE GREAT FRIENDS WITH SUCH DIFFERENT LIVES, TRYING to support each other as best they can. And they also say they're stressed! So much is going on in their words. They identified with the woman on the left; in fact, they *like* her and *like* each other. But the woman on the right? Phew! Forget her! She has nothing in common with them. She's out. They—actually, I should say we—had a great time with this conversation! We laughed. We bonded. I've mentioned this laughter and bonding *so* many times before, and now it's time we really dig in to it.

You learned in chapter 10 that, during conversation, many women create the responsible identity. *Yeah, I might sleep*, but *I'm not lazy. Yeah, I exercise*, but *I'm also OCD about my work. Everyone else's needs come before my own. And if I'm being responsible for all those needs, then there's no time to eat, sleep, rest, exercise, or enjoy life. And if I DO any of those things, it comes with a price. Because I am responsible!* Also, remember that there's a valid reason for creating this identity: If you *don't*, other women might think you're lazy. Irresponsible. Lucky. You're *out* of the club! And although we should want to be out of the club, being out leads to a new problem.

If I'm out, then I'm alone.

Here, you're going to see how much all of these themes and identities are intertwined—just like the necklaces. Recall that one outcome of girl talk is building rapport. We often engage in *troubles talk*. We create relationships and form bonds. We support and encourage. I told the story in chapter 1 of the trainers who would say, *Ladies . . . today we are going to give you an hour and a half for lunch! You can actually* chew *your food! Who in here ever gets to do that?* And then laughter and bonding ensued. Over the years, when I'm teaching, I've been a bit of an eavesdropper in restaurants, malls, and grocery stores. Here are some things I've heard:

- A group of stay-at-home moms talking about never sleeping. Then they high-five each other.
- Several working moms talking about not having enough hours in the day. They all let out a communal *Ugh!* and fall on each other laughing.
- Three women sitting together in a seminar about managing emotions, and two of them are talking about the *push, push, push at work* we've heard about before. The third says, "*Well*

why don't you just take a day off?" Woman 1 puts her arm around woman 2 and they just heehaw away! Then they *promptly* describe their chaotic lives to woman 3. (I honestly thought I was going to have to rescue woman 3! She was absolutely *out* of the club.)

This bonding isn't always bad. We need our girlfriends for that support, just like we've talked about. A great example is on YouTube. You must watch the video "I Wanna Go to Chick Fil A" by the Texting Yoga Pants (https://www.youtube.com/watch?v=qISA2TD8xhk). In the video the stay-at-home moms spend time together because: their kids are maniacs, the working moms judge them, and they can wear yoga pants, messy hair, and no makeup. It's a great example of humor and camaraderie around life's messy days!

Sometimes, however, this solidarity leads to problems—like a strong connection to being stressed-out. So a second common identity is the *I'm like you* identity. This emerges often during the discussion of the Relaxity™ ad and the Samantha vignette. I'll show you two ways the ladies presented themselves this way.

One way they created this identity was by identifying with other stressed-out women. After looking at the Relaxity ad, here's what Sondra and Jackie said about the relaxed woman on the right.

Sondra: *She looks too perfect.*

Jackie: *Yeah. I don't want to be her.*

Sondra: *She looks too together.*

This exchange is short but powerful. They talk about the woman with her act together as different, not like themselves. They concur that they would not want to be her because she's too perfect, too together. We've all done this, haven't we? And when we talk about *other* women doing this, we say it's because they're jealous, right?

This snippet actually followed a conversation about their struggles, hence *we are the same,* and *the perfect woman is different.* As before, there was laughter and nodding and *yeahs* and *mm-hmms* of validation—*yes, Sondra, you chose the right woman!* And the glances seemed to say, *Oh, that's* so *not us!* Almost all of the women identified with the frazzled-appearing woman on the left. Maybe they thought that looking like the relaxed woman would make them too different, not validated. Do you see the social evaluation thing going on here? Remember, though, there is tremendous pressure placed on women by society. The Relaxity ad still shows the woman on the right with every bit of the responsibility she had before—it's just that now she's handling it better because of an herb. She's not delegating, society's not changing the work rules, and no one's helping her more. She's just *relaxed with Relaxity!* But for those of us not taking this, we're in the club together. It's a *We* thing: *We*, (Sondra and Jackie, for example) *are alike! We. Not the Relaxity chick, but We. We are not perfect. We are frazzled and stressed but we're in it together—We.*

A second way they created the *I'm like you* identity was by first comparing their lives to other women who didn't experience the same stressors and then collaborating on their stressors together. These other women were, of course, not present. After watching the mattress commercial, I asked Carolyn and Rae if they had friends with cushy lives:

> ***Carolyn:*** *Yes. I do have one lady that . . .*
>
> ***Tami:*** *And is that a source of contention ever? As far as, like, their life versus your life, or does that ever come up?*
>
> ***Rae:*** *Not for me. My friend, her husband makes really good money so she's able to just work just because she chooses to, so she's a bookkeeper one or two days a week, just depends on how her schedule works. So no, I would never be envious, I guess. I am a little envious of it, but at the same time I'm grateful because she's in our church and she's very active and she's able to do things. She's helped me, she's picked my kids up and dressed them and taken them to dance class. I mean, she's just a miracle person. I mean, she really is, miracle woman, so even though she has it, she fills her time with volunteer work. (**Tami:** Oh. That's helpful.) Yeah.*

Carolyn: *Mine does not. My friend does not. She just seems to have no clue of the true stresses of being a parent, you know, transporting people back and forth and doing school work and all that kind of stuff, because she just, she's a stay-at-home mom, but all her kids are in school now and she just works out and (laughs) . . .*

Rae: *Oh, wow, what's that like?*

Carolyn: *Hey, you know, it's just kind of like when the rest of us are talking about, "Oh, this is crazy," you know, we've got to get our kids here and there and we've got two things scheduled on one night for the same kid, and how do you do all that, and she's just, is kind of like, "I don't get it, why are you all so stressed-out?" You know, and . . .*

Tami: *Oh, does she say that to you?*

Carolyn: *Yeah, she does.*

Tami: *And what do you say back to her?*

Carolyn: *(and we're) just like, well, we have a whole new evaluation process at school and we're trying to get this done and this done at school and she just is like, "I just don't see how that is so hard," because she's never worked outside of home (**Tami:** Mm-hmm.), she's never had a boss, and she's never had people that . . .*

Rae: *Deadlines or . . .*

Carolyn: *Yeah. So, for her it just, it doesn't make sense, and that's stressful.*

Did you notice the *we* and the *we're* and the *rest of us*? Carolyn, Rae, other working moms, and teachers are alike. Carolyn and Rae's friends are different. Carolyn describes her friend as having no clue about real stress, stating that she is just a stay-at-home mom who *just works out*. Laughter ensues as Rae jokes, *Oh, wow, what's that like?* indicating that Carolyn and Rae are alike and the friend is different. They go on to contrast *the rest of us* with the outsider, that they have jobs and bosses, which is more stress than the friend has. Before we get judgmental, let's admit that we've all done this. *I've* done it!

I can't tell you how many times I've heard the phrase *Welcome to my world!* I have to giggle because I wonder, *What does that mean? Are you excited to have me here? Do you have a welcome gift for me? Is there an orientation? Is your world awesome?* FYI, no—when someone says this, she is *not* excited, there is *not* a gift, there is *no orientation*, and her world is *not* awesome. Have I ever used the phrase? Well, of course. It's pure sarcasm. Again, if you're reading this book, I have to assume you've said it too. After watching the mattress commercial, Dalia, Lydia, and I were talking about the real world:

> ***Dalia:*** *(laughs) Welcome to my world.*
>
> ***Tami:*** *Okay. So I wondered what that means. Like, when we say it, you know, welcome to the real world or my world or, what do you think that means? What is the real world? When you say it, what do you mean?*
>
> ***Lydia:*** *I think I've said that to my sister-in-law. She's a stay-at-home mom. And every once in a while she'll just complain about being sleepy or having to do something else and I'm like, welcome to my world. I'm like, hello, that's where (laughs) . . .*
>
> ***Dalia:*** *We're like, we're like this. (laughs)*

We could have used this conversation in every single chapter so far: *Stress is the plight of women. Stress is part of living in the real world. Stress is a form of social evaluation. I'm a responsible woman.* And now *I'm like you.* Do you see it? Is it connecting? As always, there's laughter. As always, there's the back and forth of rapport. And as always, there are parts of this conversation that can't be relayed to you in a transcript, such as body language, facial expressions, and voice inflection. When Lydia said *that's where . . .* and laughed, she was gesturing to Dalia. And Dalia is right there with her as she continues the *we're like this!* Their arms were waving, their voices went up, their eyes widened with passion—*we are alike! We. Not the sister-in-law, but We. We don't sleep, but at least neither one of us sleeps. WE.*

One more conversation, from Elizabeth and Nancy. You saw a snippet of this in chapter 8, and I promised the entire conversation and that it would become even more meaningful. That time has come for the entire conversation:

Elizabeth: *Yeah, that's who she is.*

Nancy: *Because nobody's like that.*

Elizabeth: *No. And that's like, in my old neighborhood, where we used to live—we live out in the sticks now, so I don't see this, but in my old neighborhood we had that same thing, we had the women who didn't work and they would, you'd see them out, like if you had a sick day or something and you're on your way to the doctor . . .*

Nancy: *Right, or you had a kid throwing up on the floor or something.*

Elizabeth: *Yeah, you'd see them out at, like, nine thirty in the morning and they are doing their little power walk out in the neighborhood and there are two or three of them together . . .*

Nancy: *And they're just in there just dressed to the nines . . .*

Elizabeth: *. . . and they've got their little workout outfits on and . . .*

Nancy: *. . . and everything matches, the tennis shoes match.*

Elizabeth: *. . . and they're out there just . . . (laughs)*

Nancy: *If my tennis shoes don't have mud on them, I feel like I've had a good day.*

Elizabeth: *And I'm driving to the doctor going (cough cough). (laughs)*

Nancy: *Yeah. Or they'll go, "Oh, are you taking a day off?"*

Not by choice.

Tami: *Not by choice. (laughs)*

Elizabeth: *Yeah, so, yeah—that's, we had those.*

After looking at the Relaxity chick, Nancy says, *Nobody's like that!* Then they go on a back and forth that was, quite honestly, fun to experience! They finish each other's sentences. Complete each other's thoughts. They seem to be of one mind, and of course that mind is *stressed*. Cough, cough. Laugh, laugh. Back and forth. *We are alike! WE.* Not *the neighborhood women, but WE. WE have issues such as vomit, mismatched clothing, and no days off, but we're in it together. WE.* Again, notice that I was right there with them. It was all in good fun, right? Of course the bonding is therapeutic—until it sucks us into the club.

Finally, the women in my study created themselves as *alike* by co-complaining and support, but without including any other women. You've seen this conversation before, in chapter 4, when you learned about girl talk and rapport. So I'll just put a bit of it here to make the point:

Tami: *You said you need one more day?*

Grace: *Sunday afternoon I try to wrap up the laundry and it never gets totally done, you know?*

Jacqueline: *Mm-hmm. Or just clean and folded but not put away?*

Grace: *Not put away.*

Jacqueline: *Yeah.*

Grace: *On the table, and I have, maybe two more loads, I'm like, oh, I can't do this, I can't get this done.*

Jacqueline: *Yep.*

Grace: *So it's never always, all the way done . . .*

Jacqueline: *Mm-hmm.*

Grace: *. . . and so I feel like*

Jacqueline: *If you just had, if you had one more day.*

Grace: *But I'm rolling back into the week, so then it's just, like, you know, constant. Jacqueline: Yep.*

Tami: *And back again . . .*

Jacqueline: *She's my soul sister here. (laughs)*

Oh that powerful phrase, *soul sister*! Grace and Jacqueline, with very little prodding from me, talk about their weekends: cleaning house, grocery shopping, laundry, church, preparing for the next week—ugh! They try really hard to relax, but that quickly gives way to weekends filled with responsibilities. (Remember I mentioned how these all weave together?) You see lots of *mm-hmms* and questions to one another about the enormity of household chores. They conclude, together, that just one more day would solve their stress, and then Jacqueline describes Grace as her *soul sister*, accompanied by laughter. Nudging. Laughing. Lots of mm-hmms. Supporting statements. *WE are alike! WE. NOT anyone else right now, but WE.*

I don't want to leave you with the impression that these women are catty or gossipy or constant complainers. That's not what this is about. We know that women's conversations are often about rapport. We know that women tend to be more relational and that being left out feels awful—such a big risk! We know that society drives us toward living life within the confines of the Stress Club. So what's a woman to do? Remember when Alice said we're not validated if our suffering isn't the same? That means we might unknowingly adjust our conversations depending on what group we're with. We mustn't suffer more. We mustn't suffer less. We must suffer the same.

Honestly, over the course of my stressed-out life, I've had every bonding conversation with every group of women you could point to: single women, married working women without kids, married stay-at-home moms, working moms, divorced moms, blended-family moms, and empty-nest moms. Here's how some of my statements have looked in the past while talking with those groups:

- Single (in college with my friends): *Oh my gosh, people have NO idea what it's like during finals week!*
- Married, working, no kids: *Ahhhh! This job is killing me! Every day we have to work late at this place!*
- Married, stay-at-home mom: *Well, it must be nice to go off to work every day and not have someone screaming in your face all day!*
- Working mom: *She has NO idea what it's like to work all day and then have to go on "second shift" and work all night.*
- Divorced mom: *Phew, I thought I had it bad—at least they have dads to help!*
- Blended-family mom: *Single moms think they're stressed?! Try having six kids to take care of!*

Yep. I've been all of them. More specifically, I recall conversations I used to have with my teacher friends. You don't have to be a teacher to relate to this—just plug in the different departments where you work or different groups of people in your life. So we'd be at a district meeting with all grade levels—elementary, middle, and high school. Of course, we'd try to stay with the people we already knew (for me, my high school chums), but it was still easy to hear conversations from the other groups who stayed with people they knew. Here's an example of how it sometimes went:

Them—Elementary School Teachers: *Oh, ugh! I just found out our teacher's aide hours have been cut! We only get her for two hours a week. How in the world am I going to get everything done?*

Us—High School Teachers: *Teacher's Aide?! Well, that must be nice! Wish we had teacher's aides, LOL!* ☺ *Can you imagine what life would be like with actual help?*

Oh, good times. We would then do the appropriate level of eye rolling, arm slapping, and LOL-ing. We would talk about how difficult it was to plan our subject matter, how many additional responsibilities we had as high school teachers, how little help we had. You see, *we* (high school teachers) were the *same. Alike.* And *they* (elementary school teachers) were different. I am happy to say that I'm not this person anymore. I still want to commiserate with my girlfriends. I still want the bonding and support. But I *refuse* to live in a bubble where the world is forcing me into this Stress Club. I don't want to be a member.

But these are all valid concerns, you might say. I mean, teachers *do* have a lot to do. Women *do* have a lot on their plates. Women *don't often get help*. And I agree. *But* . . . remember that what we're trying to accomplish here is a missing piece of the stress puzzle. Gaining an identity within stress takes our power away. It makes our concerns ghostlike, untouchable almost. We want to bond with our girlfriends, of course. We want to support each other, certainly. And we need to be aware and careful about how we do that. We're ready for that now. It's finally time to put the pieces into the puzzle and create an exit strategy. You've been preparing for this throughout this entire book. So get ready!

More life advice from real women—Bessie and Roscoe:

Bessie: *Let's ask Roscoe for the name of her masseuse. (laughs) The first thing that comes to my mind.*

Roscoe: *Massage Envy. (laughs)*

Bessie: *I think, first of all, a lot of times people just want a good listener. People just want somebody to come in and vent on. Another woman here vented with me today about something that was obviously really stressing her out, and it was over, really, nothing, didn't have anything to do with kids or anything like that, but I just listened and I remember saying, "You know, I understand how you feel. I would feel that way, too, if somebody said that to me and that's kind of hard to take sometimes." And then she was okay. So sometimes it's a matter of just being a good listener. Sometimes it might be, make a suggestion to do something to get away from it, too.*

I'm not very good at that. I'm not good at being social with people that I work with, so . . .

Roscoe: *I agree with what Bessie is saying in that I would want to try to listen to them and ask some probing questions. You know, what is it that is causing their stress, what's going on, and then try to listen as much as I could. But then if they needed some further help I would definitely suggest further help because I kind of feel like I want to be there to listen and stuff, but yet I'm not a professional counselor, and maybe could help them a little bit better.*

Part III: Exiting the Club

Your Exit Strategy

Ginger: *I know in my own family we've had a crazy week and something that should have been very joyful, I mean, the birth of the baby? That should have been so exciting and so relaxed and so joyful, and it was not! Because we had to take time out of our schedules that were very rigid. Because we had too many things to do to go sit at the hospital. And so something, I mean, even the death that we had (laughs), it's terrible to say, but (**Tami:** We don't have time.) we don't have time! And when you don't have time to go and be with a family that is grieving, I mean. . . , something's got to give.*

I'D BE WILLING TO BET REAL MONEY THAT YOU'VE SAID THAT BEFORE: *Something's got to give!*

So why doesn't something just give, then? Why don't we rest? Why don't we relax? Why don't we sleep? Why don't we ask for help and delegate? Why don't we take time for ourselves and just exit the club? Remember, researchers are preaching that stress is killing us. We're encouraged to change our thoughts, make better choices, attend stress-management seminars, read self-help books, sleep better, or take yoga. This, they say, will lead to better stress management. But if we live with the idea that relaxation equates with laziness, if we understand that we might not be accepted by other women, then why would we attempt self-care or dare speak of it with other women who live and oftentimes wallow in stress? Over the course of this book, you've learned the answer:

IT'S TOO RISKY! WE'RE LEFT OUT OF THE CLUB! POSSIBLY LABELED AS LAZY

Once again we, women, are expected to change to fit societal expectations. And advertisers take advantage of this desire of ours to fit in. The more commercials we see with stressed-out women, the more it looks like the norm. The more we get sucked into the club. The water's getting hotter but we don't know how to jump out.

We've been looking at our stress conversations at a fundamental level. Recall that the mattress commercial, for example, contributes to our stress discussions. It does this by portraying a relaxed woman as lazy, while the rest of us are *lucky* to get six hours of sleep. The women you met here didn't hesitate to join in the chorus of judgment against the gold digger, sometimes describing her as narcissistic and without purpose. So then we feed off of that, maybe believing relaxation equals lazy. In fact, one woman said that self-care was countercultural—a great way to put it!

We navigate a bumpy terrain of word choices when we're talking with one another. We sometimes land on safe choices, and then there are other times we hit land mines! It became clear very early in my conversations with the women in my study that words such as *fantasy* and *dream world*, for example, were safe choices. Nodding, nudging, *mm-hmms*, and lots of support occurred with these words. And the land mines? Phrases such as *Oh yes, I do sleep* were not safe. These were met with, *Well, you must not have a lot going on!*

YIKES! IT'S TOO RISKY! YOU LEFT ME OUT! YOU CALLED ME LAZY!

I hope I've opened your eyes to this weird, up until now unknown terrain we've been traversing. How can we begin to better understand what stress means to us if we're unaware of this hidden world? In this realm, we construct our identities—who we are. This is the big, hidden piece of the puzzle: our identities. Only recently has identity been seen as something that can change between or even within conversations, because identity is simply who we are to each other. So we *can* change who we want to be and who we are. We *can* forfeit our memberships in this destructive, all-consuming club.

The fabulous women in my study replied to an email asking for women who identified themselves as stressed-out. Most of them described stress as bad, but then constructed themselves as stressed during our conversations. That makes us ask: Why do women continually choose to describe themselves as stressed-out when they know that stress is a bad thing? Why admit it—why admit this predilection to consistently allow something in our lives that is bad? The pull to be *responsible* and *alike* appears to be so strong that talking about not sleeping, running nonstop, and being stressed-out was safe. The suffering was the same, so all was good.

Going even deeper, remember the spot-on description of women *joining voices of past and present*? If conversations about stress are seen as ongoing and historical, then our current stress talk could be a carryover from times when women were *not* seen as responsible, contributing members of society. Maybe we have an underlying fear of being identified by others as lazy, not productive, or not as valuable members of society. Who wants that!

As I mentioned in the introduction, before I started this research I described women as using their stress as a means to martyr themselves, like they were gaining a type of self-importance. Now it is clear that wasn't what was happening! It wasn't that women were making martyrs of themselves; rather, they were creating themselves in ways acceptable to society. To speak otherwise presented risk and left them alone and feeling judged.

Until we take exception to the way advertisers and the media send different messages to women regarding stress, change will be a challenge. Seminars on stress need to be changed, rewritten. Even seminar leaders conducting stress-training sessions talk about women as stressed. Remember the line, *Ladies . . . today we are giving you an hour and a half for lunch! You can actually* chew *your food! Who in here* ever *gets to do that?!* Remember the laughter, nudging, and *Amens* as the women enacted both the *I'm responsible* and the *I'm like you* identities? We need to be aware of the messages we're seeing and hearing as well as how we react to them. You can begin to ask yourself questions like, *Am I OK with a life that never allows me to chew my food? Will I continue to sit in this pot of now boiling water that has felt normal for years? Or will I be a part of the revolution, take my power back, and start living my own life?*

It won't be easy. I don't want to minimize how countercultural this new way of life will be; the struggle is real. Women struggle with the conflict between knowing they should take care of themselves versus actually doing it. In chapter 4, I told you about Ideological Dilemmas, those internal struggles that often are manifested in the words that we speak. I heard the impasse these women experienced through their words! They all talked about stress as the plight of women, as a reality of living in the real world, and as a form of social evaluation. Through their stress talk, they all presented themselves as responsible and alike. Yet they all answered yes when I asked if it was important to take care of themselves. And if they *did* take care of themselves in some way, they were quick to explain how that did not make them lazy and to point out the consequences of telling others about their self-care.

We'll start formulating your plan in just a bit. First, though, I want you to see the words that indicate this internal conflict between living a happy life and mitigating the risk it poses. As always I want you to self-reflect. Take time to consider how *you* might have responded if you had been included in the conversations you've seen in this book.

Let's return to Jacqueline and Grace. When you read these words, look for everything we've talked about: women, the real world, social evaluation, responsibility, and sameness. Then notice their final exchanges and the struggle that's taking place:

Grace: *I've said, "Well, in my world," you know . . . (laughs)*

Tami: *What would that mean? Like, what you think that's all about.*

Grace: *Well, I guess people like that lady don't really live in the real world? Because they don't have to deal with daily stress, you know? They have housekeepers and people working for them and take on so many of the stresses.*

Jacqueline: *And if they do feel stressed, they have time, they can afford to pay to get a massage. Or a facial. Or a pedicure. Like, those luxuries that, like those beauty luxuries, I feel like that's one of the things that I am most jealous of. You know? If I see a woman who looks pretty and put together, then I'm just like, well she doesn't work where I work. (laughs) (**Grace:** Right, she doesn't, you know . . .*

Grace: *She's not working full time with kids at home, that's for sure.*

Jacqueline: *She has time and money, maybe a rich man behind her who can afford to pay for all these little spa treatments.*

Grace: *Right.*

Jacqueline: *Like then I just kind of, it makes me feel kind of jealous. (laughs)*

Grace: *But I wouldn't trade it, you know, I would rather live in the real world than a (**Jacqueline:** Right.) pretentious, fake world. (**Jacqueline:** Right.) You know? But I think in the real world to me is when you do your own work, in a way? (**Jacqueline:** Mm-hmm. (laughs)*

Then later:

Tami: *Well, tell me, do you think it's important as women that we do take care of ourselves?*

Jacqueline: *It is. And we don't.*

Grace: *It is.*

Tami: *Okay, so tell—at all?*

Jacqueline: *Hardly. I barely do.*

Then a few minutes later:

Jacqueline: *Like, I have just been kind of just saying forget it, I'm going to just relax right now. (**Grace:** Right.) Like, I'm not taking any work home. If it doesn't get done here, it's just not getting done, and I have made peace with that. But, it doesn't decrease the stress that much, because then I still feel guilty.*

Do you hear the struggle in their words?
I'm jealous of the relaxed life.
But I wouldn't want it.
My stress is part of me. It's the real world.
But I wouldn't want to be a part of the fake world.
Real world women don't have time to take care of themselves.
But I need to take care of myself.
But I don't.
But sometimes I do.
And then I feel guilty.
And precious Candy! In chapter 6 I mentioned how women's brains are constantly active.

How's this for active!

Candy: *I try. (laughs) I am trying to get into shape and, just the normal stuff. . . . there's things that's part of my routine to try and get another thing accomplished and I've been listening to my daughter, for her and I to get in shape together. So, I mean, we do that, but it's another thing that's not getting done, because I'm so busy that, eight o'clock I'm so tired (**Tami:** Yeah.) that I can't do it, so, I think I take that hour, or half-hour, whatever it is that I put my kids to sleep and I just, I get on Facebook and I just check it out for a little bit, kind of something that I don't have to think about and probably spend ten minutes reading a book. I almost finished that book that you gave me [to Ginger]. And in the morning I have no idea how much time I take, probably thirty minutes to fifteen,*

> *roughly in there somewhere, to do a Bible study or whatever happens to be going on at the time (***Tami:** *Mm-hmm.), because between reading the book and doing that in the morning, I am much calmer throughout the day and not as affected by things, you know?*

Bless her heart!
I'm trying to get into shape with my daughter.
I am getting into shape.
I mean, we do, but no, we don't.
I get on Facebook. An hour. No, half an hour.
I do a Bible study in the mornings. Thirty minutes. No, fifteen. Or maybe not a Bible study. Depends.
After all this, I'm calmer throughout the day.

She does not seem one bit calmer! I'm not making fun—really, I'm not. It's just that I can see myself being the voice of this long string of words And I'm guessing you can, too. And it's such a struggle! My hope is that by this time you can pick out where the pressure is being expressed as you hear them talk. And *ugh!* How exhausting to deal with this internal struggle. Especially when you haven't even been aware that it exists, and so you didn't know you could work on it.

Now you have enlightenment. The blinders have been lifted. Recall we need a *revolution of our minds*! You know now that you are the only one in your world who is going to take your power back. Your families and friends can't do it for you. Colleagues, bosses, employees, and social groups can't do it for you; only you can. So you should now be in the mind-set to stop participating in this debilitating club, and hopefully you've been transforming as you have followed along.

What do I mean by an exit strategy? I'll start with a visual, which you can see on the next page.

Here's what you're up against. We're surrounded by societal messages that tell us we're stressed, stressed, stressed. Television sitcoms depict women living like maniacs. Researchers tell us life is crazy. And take a minute to visit a magazine rack around the holidays to

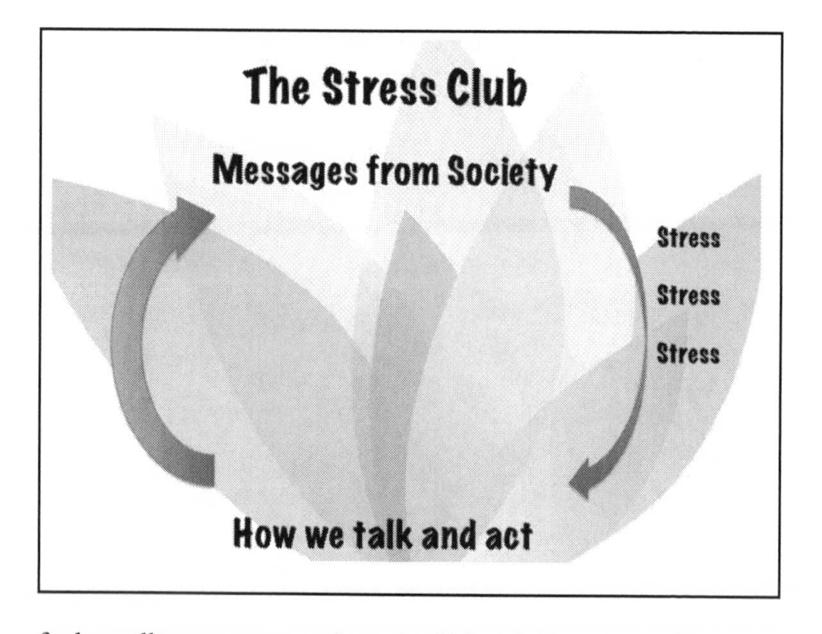

find a million ways to *not* be overwhelmed: *Ten ways to keep your stress down over the holidays and still be the best-dressed woman in your ladies group even if you've gained fifteen pounds while making our low-stress holiday candies. Bust your stress while making buttery yummy homemade Christmas cookies that you can hand paint while you're waiting in the carpool line or on the train home from work. How to make delicate, beautiful, uniquely individual Thanksgiving place settings and still have plenty of time to sleep (for a few minutes, LOL)*! Of course I made these up, but you know what I mean; you've seen these headlines. But not to worry: there are products for all of your busyness, even during the holidays. And you'll often find these products in the same magazine that's telling you not to be stressed, sending mixed messages. There's a mattress to help you sleep better, an herbal supplement to help you relax, and deodorant for stress sweat because, according to advertisers, stress sweat is different from regular sweat. Oh malarkey! Sweat is sweat!

This is how we initially become part of a club we didn't know existed. We see these messages every single day. We see very successful women running themselves into the ground. We feel the pressure. Stress now seems normal. Frenzied lives and unhappiness seem like the only way. What happens after this craziness starts feeling normal? What happens is, well, everything you've learned in this book. Now, we get together with our friends and *talk* about our crazy, busy, stressful lives. We talk about stress as the plight of women. We talk about the *real world*—that stress is inevitable and unavoidable. We talk about stress and then evaluate each other's level of suffering. Remember: you must suffer! And when you talk in these ways, you are saying something to your friends about who you are: *you are responsible* (I mean, after all, you are running nonstop twenty-four hours a day, seven days a week.) and *you are just like all of your friends* (high-five, girlfriend!). Doesn't this sound exhausting? No wonder you are so tired.

Two situations I just experienced. First, I was having lunch with a friend recently and she asked me if my book was going to teach women self-care, like meditation. Then, the next day I was presenting this topic, "The Stress Club," at a women's meeting. When I walked in, a group asked me if I was going to teach them how to de-stress; then they laughed, nudged, and high-fived one another. I hope you have an idea of the answer to both of these questions: it's *NO*. I'm not here to teach you self-care or de-stressing techniques, although I will guide you in the importance of both. If I were to do that, you would be getting the same thing from this book that you've gotten from every other book, magazine, and website about stress. I would be saying to you, *Phew, we do have it rough as women! Let me show you how to manage your stress.* My mission is different.

You're close to putting this book down and rejoining the world. You will continue to see and hear stress messages in the media. You and your friends will gather and chat. So what I *am* here to do is help you interact with this world. I'm here to guide you, not in stress management, but in identity management (just thought of that phrase—love it!). I'm here to encourage you to pay attention to that stress deodorant commercial and then decide if you buy into the message. I'm here to encourage you to be aware of the language you're using, how you're using it, and to change what you'd like to change. Then you'll be able to choose between participating in the club and participating in your own life—even during times when it's a challenging life! This is what I mean by an exit strategy.

If what I've taught you in the last eleven chapters is true, then how do you even begin this exit? It's a process. Recall the promise I made to you in the Introduction: *If you decide to read this book, if you choose to believe it, if you really do the activities, if you practice, and if you give it time, your life* will *change. I promise!* Well, you've read the book. Do you believe it? If so, it's time to do the work, practice, and allow time for your life to be yours.

Let's get to work!

Puzzle Piece No. 1: Your Identity

The first step in disconnecting from stress forever is to *decide* (love this word, by the way) who you are. Why start here? Because this is the concept that makes this book different from other stress books: the connection between stress and your identity. You've learned that *stressed-out* is an identity. Just like being a daughter is an identity, being calm or assertive or kind or confident are all identities. We start here so that you can be in charge of who you are. Don't let your identity be a secret to you. Don't allow society to tell you who you are. Stop letting some faceless voice on a car commercial tell you that he knows you have to get up early, work late, and never sleep in between (remember the car commercial from chapter 10?). Yes, I realize we have seasons of life where we have more responsibility than others. I'm aware that some days are more challenging than others. I understand that if you have a baby or a spouse or child with the flu, you're going to lose sleep for a time. But overall, decide who you want to be and what type of life you'd like to have. This might sound like a major rant, but I am done with having hundreds, probably thousands, of nameless, faceless advertisers tell me who I should be and that I am not supposed to rest or enjoy life. I will decide for myself, thank you very much.

One more rant before you work on your strategy. I want to be clear that this book is not permission to become lazy and annoying. Hmm—how do I say this without sounding judgmental? Here goes:

In chapter 2 you learned that we are social creatures and most absorbed in life when we are part of something bigger than ourselves. In chapter 9 you learned that in order to survive as a society, people must serve the needs of one another. In chapter 10 I proposed that we were created to be productive, to work (whatever work is for you) and to help others. I've encountered women along my journey who, after years of counseling, self-help, and self-reflection, stop participating in this *pack* style of life. They have been so programmed with concepts like *me time*, *self-care*, and *inner peace*, that they often forget about those around them. They become so *me* oriented that they lose their sense of connectedness. This is not my intent in engaging you in this exit strategy. My intent is to help you become aware of the stress messages being fed to you and to give you the tools to help you decide whether or not you will participate in the madness. Yes, I want you to take care of yourself and enjoy life. But, no, I don't want you to be the only focus of your existence. That approach doesn't seem to lead to a fulfilling life.

Rant's over. On to your work.

Tool No. 1: Who are you?

In chapter 9 you learned about the concept of identity. Part of your identity involves those descriptors that are fairly easy to classify—who you *are*. Check all that describe you. The list is not exhaustive, of course, so I've added some lines for you to add others.

___ Sister
___ Spouse
___ Aunt
___ Niece
___ Mother
___ Grandmother
___ Working mom
___ Stay-at-home mom
___ Single
___ Daughter
___ Spouse

___ Engaged
___ Divorced
___ Widowed
___ Employee/Boss/Colleague (specify or write in others)

____

____

____

____

____

This is a great starting point! It forces you to think about how complex you are. It gives you some structure to realize how many roles you fill and how awesome you are. Be careful, though, if you happen to be overflowing with checkmarks and words: don't take that as *proof* that you are stressed. Practice your newfound awareness of the overuse of that word by saying your life is *abundant*.

Checking boxes and writing descriptions of yourself might seem like fairly objective activities. But are they? I'll be bold and say that *all* of the descriptors that you marked or wrote down are more complex than they appear. Let's go deeper.

Tool No. 2: How do you think about yourself?

Another part of your identity involves how you think about yourself. I was bold before and said these are more than just words. The identity of *daughter*, for example, would mean very little to you if your parents weren't available to you and you were raised in foster homes. The word might conjure thoughts of low self-worth or of not being valued. *Daughter* might mean something entirely different to you if you were raised with loving parents (or by a mother who guilted you!). Depending on your background, you might think of yourself as a:

- Good daughter
- Responsible daughter

- Caring or loving daughter
- Horrible daughter (Let's just be real here! Whatever they are, your words should be honest.)

A. On the lines below, write the identities you checked above in Tool No. 1, and then write how you *think* about yourself within that identity. You can write single descriptive words like I did above with *daughter*. Or you can write sentences detailing your thoughts (as I did below with *spouse*). Make sure you describe how you think you are, not how you want to be (if there's a difference).

Here's an example for *spouse* to guide you if you're writing a longer description:

> ***Spouse:*** *I am a great spouse most of the time. I am thoughtful, respectful, and loving. I try to pick my battles and argue well. Sometimes I don't speak up in order to avoid conflict. I'm better now and still working on it.*

____

____

____

____

____

B. Finally, take some time to read each description and decide if how you are meshes with how you want to be. If not, write a description for how you'd *like* to be on the lines below. Then, if you want to make changes, jot down some ideas on how to be that person. Below is my description of how I think I am as an aunt versus how I'd like to be.

Aunt*—how I think I am: I'm nice, but not very involved. Sometimes I feel awkward. When I'm with my nieces, sometimes it's like I'm just a friend of their mom's—my fault, not theirs.*

Aunt*—how I'd like to be: I'd like to be that fun person they call when they have a problem. I'd like to be able to guide them and give them advice.*

How I can be that person: I do want to make some changes. One of my nieces is going to college soon, so I'll start by sending her regular texts to see how she's doing.

____

____

____

____

How does this help you exit the club? Going deeper, recall that this part of who you are isn't necessarily factual. I had you describe how you felt about your roles because those words are also parts of your identity and they can change—they *are* dependent on what we think. When we don't spend time reflecting on how we think about ourselves, then it's a mystery. We become shaped by thoughts we don't even know exist, and sometimes we even have an identity we wish was different. And when these internal conflicts occur, we call them *stressful*. This activity helps you identify discrepancies between who you are and what you want to be, and then to consider your choices. We have one more activity to do in this section.

C. Here's more of the *Time Magazine* article I mentioned in chapter 9 for you to read:

Among the most confounding changes of all is the evidence, tracked by numerous surveys, that as women have gained more freedom, more education and more economic power, they have become less happy. . . . It may be that women have become more honest about what ails them. Or that they are now free to wrestle with the same pressures and conflicts that once accounted for greater male unhappiness. Or that modern life in a global economy is simply more stressful for everyone but especially for women, who are working longer hours while playing quarterback at home.[16]

Seems straightforward, but answer a few questions:

1. Do you feel you are more or less happy than women of earlier years?
2. How do you feel about the idea that you are less happy because you now wrestle with the same issues that make men unhappy?
3. Do you feel life in a global economy makes life more stressful for you?
4. Does this extract describe how you feel about yourself? Explain.

Become a critical reader. Don't just take all messages about life at face value. Question if the messages reflect how *you* feel about yourself. This is a great way to transition into the last part of the identity section. This study cites how women feel unhappy, and then speculates on why we might feel this way. During your time spent in the Stress Club, you would probably have read something like this and not considered whether or not you choose to be a participant. You may have read it as validation of your stressed-out life. As you proceed through your exit strategy, red flags should start waving like crazy any time you read an article that describes women. The flags are there to alert you: *Do I feel this way about myself? Will I participate in this club activity of feeling unhappy? Or will I make the decision that I am going to live my own life, not the concept of life that's been crammed down my throat all these years?*

This brings us to the final part of your identity exercises, the world!

Tool No. 3: How the world thinks about you.

After reading the article below, describe this woman. Just jot down the thoughts that come to mind, whether the thoughts are just words or complete sentences. Try to comment on multiple aspects of her story: her own description of her life, what she wants to do with her day, why she can't do it, who keeps her from doing it, etc.

Reader Rant: I Need a Day All to Myself

When her "me day" goes awry, one mom tries to salvage her sense of self.

By Marlene Arute

I love my two kids and my job, but sometimes I need a break—not an hour folding laundry, but a day just for me. As everything started to go wrong, I wondered: Can this "me day" be saved?

For months I've been attempting to take some time for myself. But something always got in the way: a crisis at work, a neighbor's barbecue, a sick kid. I wasn't going for anything epic, like a spa weekend with the girls. As a mom of two who works long hours as an event planner, I just needed a day to jump off the runaway train that is my life and restore a bit of energy and perspective. I was thinking a manicure, a little shopping, even a movie. This was part of a vow I'd made after a false-alarm health scare to take better care of myself. Realizing that I live in a constant state of trying to catch up, keep in touch and get where I'm supposed to be, I began plotting my "me day." Here's how it turned out.

12:06 A.M. I hit Send on a sick-day email to work. I would have taken a personal day but didn't want to risk my boss denying my request. After fabricating a food-poisoning story, I dream about which color nail polish I'll choose.

5:27 A.M. My four-year-old has to go to the bathroom. "I can't go unless you tell me a story." He outright rejects my offer of one million dollars to go solo.

5:37 to 7:30 A.M. I can't fall back to sleep, so I decide to get an early start on my special day. A blur of pouring cereal, packing lunches and finding missing shoes is punctuated by a "Hey, you're not dressed" from my husband. "I'm taking the day," I say as I shove him out the door. Silence. My "me day" has begun. I enjoy a cup of coffee and flip through the newspaper.

8:01 A.M. My BlackBerry vibrates. "I know you don't feel well but . . . " writes my boss. Flower arrangements for a client breakfast are MIA.

8:02 to 9:31 A.M. I chase down the flowers, listen to an angry client and switch off the BlackBerry.

9:45 A.M. I arrive at the nail salon and select Hot Mamma red. My nails are still wet when the call comes from the principal.

10:05 to 10:15 A.M. I listen to the details of my eleven-year-old's detention-worthy deed. A promise of proper punishment gets me off the phone, but my nails are smudged.

12:30 P.M. Dreams of a leisurely lunch are smashed when my friend Kristen pleads too much paperwork.

1:00 to 3:12 P.M. A call to a backup friend backfires. As she rants about how crazy her life is, I polish off a jar of peanut butter.

4:20 P.M. I head to the mall. A cute dress makes me look like a horse, so I skip shopping for a spin class.

6:03 P.M. I listen to the seven voicemails my husband has left with a laundry list of chores since "you're taking a day and have some free time."

6:07 P.M. Fantasizing about being single, I call my husband to remind him that he's in charge of homework, dinner, baths, and bedtime.

7:00 P.M. The only movie not sold out is in 3-D. I pass.

7:10 P.M. I buy a bunch of daffodils, a bottle of sauvignon blanc, and a romantic comedy DVD before heading home.

9:02 P.M. I refill my glass, giggle at the antics of Sandra Bullock and congratulate myself on salvaging my "me day." I'll book another—soon. Because if something's gotta give, it's not going to be me.

(Reprinted with permission from Marlene Arute, the author)

____

____

____

____

Was this a test? Yes. Did I trick you? Maybe. You've actually already met Marlene. I introduced her story in chapter 10, and mentioned some responses to her rant from women tuning in to one of my webinars: *stressed, busy, selfish, ridiculous thinking she should have time for herself, lazy, high strung, busy, stressed, at her breaking point.* My hope here was you would remember that and then not be too critical of her in writing, even if you were only doing it to try to say the right thing. I was hoping your thoughts are changing now and that it would feel wrong to condemn her for wanting a day of fun.

Recall from chapter 11 that sometimes we talk about our stress as a form of social evaluation. Simply put, we judge each other. Of course, it works both ways: we judge, and we also know we are being judged. So you can imagine that Marlene's feelings about herself, her identity, and what activities she might be able to get away with are all influenced by what others think of her. And so are yours. If you can practice being less judgmental of women like Marlene, even if it's just in words for now, then you will be less likely to be affected by judgments about who you are.

We do live in a complicated world—I'll give you that! We have and we create many identities each day as we exist and interact with others. This can make life exciting and full. It can also make life miserable & unfulfilling if we aren't aware of our identities and how they're influenced by what we think and what others say about us.

Having an awareness of your multiple personalities (☺) is foundational to your exit strategy. I don't know how you progressed through these activities, i.e., what you wrote, how you described yourself, or how you judge or feel about being judged by the world. If who you are is a mystery to you, then you'll be influenced by thoughts you don't even realize you're having. *(I'm a woman, so life sucks. The real world is awful—we all just have to deal with it. I must be busy and fit in with my stressed-out friends.)* You'll be susceptible to the judgments of others (*Wow! Must be nice that you have time to read! Ha!*) And you'll likely become a Platinum Member of the Stress Club, sitting in that boiling pot of water!

I say NO! So let's go on to the next piece of the puzzle.

Puzzle Piece No. 2: Your Girl Talk

You've completed Puzzle Piece No. 1, various exercises and self-assessments to help you determine who you are. This puzzle piece is designed to help you decide what word choices you'll make in conversation—especially with other women.

The field of discursive psychology is based upon the premise that we *do* something when we talk. For purposes of the Stress Club, what we do when we talk is tell each other that we're stressed, and therefore responsible and like one another. Do a quick mental check of your work in the last section: Did you write down *stressed-out* as an identity you'd like to have? I'm guessing no (although who knows). Now it's time to work on the identities you *do* want to have.

For example, two of the identities I want to create for myself are *wise* and *emotionally mature*. Phew, now that's a challenge! I want to be a good example for my children and the people I lead. I want to walk out my life such that, despite challenges, I don't become tied to a stressed-out identity. Now, this does not mean I'm the *rose-colored glasses* kind of gal. If I tell you I'm going through something and you say, *Oh gosh, I'm sorry!*, you won't hear me say back, *Oh no it's all good! The sun is shining and I'm blessed just to not be dead.* I'll be real when things are hard. But what I will not do is huff and sigh and wallow just because I may have to get up early, get to the airport, fly all day, and get to my hotel late. After years of working on this myself, it finally feels fairly natural to alter my talk. How can you get to that same place?

Examine Your Talk

A. Your Identity Talk

First, let's examine your talk that tells others who you are. I just went through the first eleven chapters and made a list of some of the words and phrases that were used by the stressed-out women in my study as well as those I've heard from women over the last ten years of training. These are the phrases that gave them the appearance of *responsible* and *I'm like you*. Examine them:

1. *I can't/I have to!*
2. *Must be nice.*
3. *Lucky you!*
4. *Well, at least you . . .*
5. *You have no idea/People don't understand!*
6. *Welcome to my world/Join the club!*
7. *You think YOU'RE stressed!*
8. Lucky you!
9. Well in the *real world*!
10. Who in here *ever* gets to (insert whatever activity, like *chew your food*)?
11. Just wait till you (again, insert whatever activity, like *have kids*).
12. I surely can't be doing better than you in (insert area, like *getting enough sleep).*
13. Well, you must not have a lot going on!
14. I would never have time to sit there and (fill in the activity, like *think about things*).
15. I feel guilty because (whatever you did to take care of your-self).
16. She's my soul sister! (cause we're both hysterically crazy)
17. She doesn't work where I work!
18. Sounds like a dream world!
19. I'd like to be her!
20. Wish I had time to watch a movie!
21. Hard day? Welcome to my world.
22. I'm OCD.
23. I'm a perfectionist.

24. Yes, I get enough sleep at night, but I'm not lazy.
25. You have twelve things on your list? Quick slacking–I have like twenty!
26. My friend has no clue of true stress because she's never (fill in, like *had a job*)

Did this elicit any emotions to see them all here at once? It did for me. Did some resonate with you more than others? Did you find yourself thinking *Oh goodness, I say that one all the time?*

Since I keep telling you this type of talk is not conducive to a happy life, I'd better give you some alternatives. It's going to feel weird at first. It will take time to feel comfortable out of the club when your girlfriends are still in. But you are a rebel! No one is going to force you into an unfulfilling life anymore! Hear you roar! This time, with conscious intent! Starting on the following page are some suggestions; sometimes the suggestion will be simply not to say it.

What should you do with this? How do you incorporate it into your life? I try to be flexible in giving long-term assignments. We all approach self-assessment differently, so below are a couple of options. Try to focus on your words for at least one full week, but longer is better!

1. You could simply make mental notes. Commit these negative phrases or these types of phrases to memory. Then notice when, where, why, and with whom you use them. The *why* comes from everything you have studied so far. Is it because you were with your friends and didn't want to risk being left out? I realize there are other reasons you may have for using these phrases—only you can assess what those reasons are. Of course, the list is only a fraction of those that women might use, so be aware of others as well. By this point in your stress study you should be capable of picking them out. Each time, consider some of the alternative responses from above.

Your Identity Talk

The Old Phrase	A Better Way
I can't!	***That's not a good option for me.***
I have to!	***I think it's best if I do this.***
Must be nice/ Lucky you!	***That's great!*** *(be careful about a sarcastic tone.)*
Well at least you... *(insert comparison like "don't have to be at work as early as I do!")*	**Gosh, that sounds rough too.**
You have no idea/ People don't understand!	***I'm feeling very upset about...***
Welcome to my world/ Join the club!	***Sounds like we're experiencing the same thing.***
You think YOU'RE stressed!	***Gosh, that sounds rough too.***
Lucky you!	***That's great!*** *(be careful about a sarcastic tone.)*
Well in the REAL world!	***In my experience...***
Who in here EVER gets to... *(insert area like "chew your food")*	***Let's have a relaxing lunch today!***
Just wait till you... *(insert activity like "have kids!")*	***I remember when I was in your season of life. I enjoyed it very much, and I love this one too.***

Your Identity Talk (cont)

The Old Phrase	A Better Way
Well, you must not have a lot going on!	***That's great!*** *(be careful about a sarcastic tone.)*
I would never have time to sit there and... *(fill in the activity like "think about things!")*	***I would love to be able to do that, but I struggle. How do you make it work?***
I feel guilty because I... *(whatever you did to take care of yourself like "read for an hour.")*	*(Just don't say it! I have a 5-minute lesson on guilt at tamiwest.com/videos; scroll to find "Tami Guilt.mov" in the video list.)*
I surely can't be doing better than you in... *(insert area like "getting enough sleep"!)*	***I'm happy to share my sleep secrets.***
She's my soul sister! *(because we're both hysterically crazy)*	***It's ok to use this phrase. Just try to use it to bond over something other than stress.***
Well, she obviously doesn't work where I work!	***Sounds like a nice place to work.***
Sounds like a dream world to me!	***That sounds very nice.***
I'd love to be her!	***She seems happy. Maybe I'll model some of the things she does.***

Your Identity Talk (cont)

The Old Phrase	A Better Way
Wish I had time to watch a movie!	***I've wanted to see a movie for months. I'm going to plan it!***
Hard day? Welcome to my world!	***Hard day? Can I help?***
I'm OCD!	***I'm dedicated to what I do.***
I'm a perfectionist!	***I'm dedicated to what I do.***
Yes, I get enough sleep at night, but I'm not lazy!	***I know our bodies need sleep.***
You have 12 things on your list? Quick slacking! I have like 20 on mine!	***Goodness, 12 things? That's a lot.***
My friend has no clue about true stress because she's never… *(insert activity like "had a job!")*	***We have different lives and different challenges.***

2. Another option is to copy or duplicate the chart on the following page and keep up with your words. You'll note, as above, when, where, why, with whom you use them, and how you could respond differently next time. Notice the extra lines for phrases or words not included here.

B. Your Stress Talk

Now let's look at ways to actually eliminate the word *stress* from your vocabulary. In chapter 5, I provided a few responses to the question, *What is stress?* I've listed them below. Remember, all of these women were in the club. And those in the club say they're stressed. Throughout this book I have talked about eliminating the word "stress" from your vocabulary. Well then you're going to need some replacement words. Let's do some analysis of these words and see if we can make some changes. What we're going to do is try to have our laser focused mental pointers scanning our words for real issues. Grouping everything that happens to you under that one umbrella word, stress, takes your power away. It hinders you from figuring out what's really bothering you. When you say you're stressed, you're actually just grouping things. As you make your exit, try trading an emotion for the word stress. For example, maybe you have a teenage daughter who comes home late nearly every night and you say it's making you stressed-out! What you might really be feeling is anger that she's being disobedient. Or maybe you're feeling worried every night that something's happened. Now that you've identified the issue, you can make choices to work on those parts of your life. The final part of your exit strategy involves those choices, but I'll throw some things in here to get you started. Let's suggest some word substitutions and give these girls some power back!

1. **Kate:** *So that's stressful, I mean, I get up at five o'clock in the morning, leave my daughter all day, and don't even know how I'm going to make ends meet, so, . . .*

   a. It sounds like Kate is tired (a more specific word than stressed) of getting up at 5 A.M. Should she go to bed earlier? If so, she might need to train her kids to do the same. She might

Tracking Your Word Choices

Word or Phrase	When	Where	Why	With Whom	Next time I could say…

have to let go of some household perfectionism and get her family to help.

b. She seems disturbed (another more specific word—you get the picture of how I'm doing this, so I'll stop the parentheses.) that she leaves her daughter all day. She might need to explore her feelings about being a working mom. If that's what she really wants, she could find role models who have done it successfully. Many do. What she should not do is compare herself to stay-at-home moms. What if she really doesn't want to work and leave her daughter? It's time to explore finances, etc. Again, she could find role models who've done it. She'll need to decide if she can let go of the working woman identity for a time.

c. It appears she is worried about finances, not knowing if she'll make ends meet. Has she had a Come to Jesus meeting with her husband? Are there changes that can and should be made?

I'll do one more, and then ask you to do the other three.

2. Racecar: *Car problems, your air-conditioning unit went out . . .*

It sounds like Racecar's problems are varied: worried about finances (not enough money to fix these things), frustrated due to a lack of knowledge (doesn't know how to fix these things), or maybe she's simply irritated that she has to mess with it at all. Life is going to be filled with broken cars and A/Cs, right? She'll need to pinpoint exactly what the problem is.

Now it's your turn. Try doing the same thing with Bernie and Pebbles.

3. Bernie: *Working in high school, you're working with teenagers, and big sources of stress for me are teenagers who don't seem to be held accountable for their behavior.*

____

____

____

4. Pebbles: *See, all that stuff is monetary, too. I think stress really does go back to that as a core. And I hate to say that, but there is a lot of even with my aging parents. That's my real concern. . . . I know that their health is what their health is and obviously I am concerned about their health and wanting them to stay healthy as long as possible, but it's the money. Are we going to have enough money. . . ?*

____

____

____

____

5. Pebbles: *I think that that's it, sometimes it becomes so overwhelming that I fold and collapse and give up. I can't get it all done anyway, so I might as well not even try. Sometimes that does occur when it becomes so overwhelming. But I think for the most part, most normal stressful days are just normal lifedays . . .*

____

____

____

____

Sometimes when I teach seminars about the Stress Club I have women create a list of emotions and words they can use instead of stress. Here's a conglomeration of words, and in some cases phrases, they've come up with over the years:

overwhelmed
anxious
frustrated
worried
annoyed
concerned
exhausted
pressured
tired
disappointed
overworked
confused
depressed
discouraged
panicked
pissed
busy
emotional
hungry
insecure
irate
irritated
livid
overloaded
sad
abandoned
afraid
aggravated
agitated
alone
behind
brain-dead
bummed
burdened
challenged
chaotic
defeated
deflated
disillusioned
drained
driven
dumbfounded
enraged
fatigued
fearful
fed up
flustered
frazzled
fried
frightened
hands are tied
I have had it up to here
ignored
imperfection
inadequate
invisible
jarred
lack of control
lethargic
misunderstood
nervous
overly sensitive
overpromised
overwrought

pained
perplexed
physically challenged
powerless
put off
quiet
stretched thin
tapped out
time management challenged
trapped
traumatized
ugh
unappreciated
unaware
uncertain
undermined
underpaid
unhappy
unprepared
used

Add your own. And now, each time you say *I'm stressed-out*, catch yourself and use this list.

I have to say though, as I read through the list it struck me as a little bit of a depressing way to end this section. Of course, it's fabulous to have so many specific emotions to choose from to replace the word stress. But I also want you to have some words to describe the positive parts of your life. So here are a few from a great website, https://www.englishclub.com/vocabulary/adjectives-personality-positive.htm.

adaptable
adventurous
affable
affectionate
agreeable
ambitious
amiable
amicable
amusing
brave
bright
broad-minded
calm
careful
charming
communicative
compassionate
conscientious
considerate
convivial
courageous
courteous
creative
decisive
determined
diligent
diplomatic
discreet

dynamic
easygoing
emotional
energetic
enthusiastic
exuberant
fair-minded
faithful
fearless
forceful
frank
friendly
funny
generous
gentle
good
gregarious
hard-working
helpful
honest
humorous
imaginative impartial
independent
intellectual
intelligent
intuitive
inventive
kind
loving
loyal
modest
neat
nice
optimistic
passionate
patient
persistent
pioneering
philosophical
placid
plucky
polite
powerful
practical
proactive
quick-witted
quiet
rational
reliable
reserved
resourceful
romantic
self-confident
self-disciplined
sensible
sensitive
shy
sincere
sociable
straightforward
sympathetic
thoughtful
tidy
tough
unassuming
understanding
versatile
warmhearted
willing
wise
witty

Love, love, love this list! We have so much power with the words we use. And so *many* words to choose from. As you read the list, you'll probably find some you love and some that make you go *eck*! And that's fine. Just remember to not only focus on and identify the difficult situations in your life, but also to pay attention to the great ones.

The Final Puzzle Piece: Taking Care of Yourself

We could have stopped with the second puzzle piece and you would be well on your way out of the club. Those sections are what make this plan different. By now you and your identity should be pretty chummy. Your word choices should be annoying you. *What?* You ask. I mean there might now be a little voice in your head reminding you not to tell your friend she's lucky to have taken a day off. The voice will never go away now. You're welcome. *And* you're probably noticing all the advertisements that tell you how crappy your life is and how it could be so much better if you would just go shopping! So I could have stopped there, but I'm going to end with the final activity, mainly as an encouragement to you.

During the *Stress Club* sessions I mentioned in the last section, I also ask women to create a list of self-care ideas. The directions are simple:

With the women at your table, come up with a list of ways to manage your stress (yes, I say it this way because it's early in the seminar and they don't know yet that the word stress is about to exit their vocabularies!). Be as creative or as boring as you'd like.

Then I give them five minutes. Starting on the next page, here's the list (I kept it in their own words, even if they sounded silly—many of them have made me laugh over the years):

Remember chapter 4 on Girl Talk and how it taught you about one view in which women *do* friendship simply by talking. Notice how many of these self-care ideas include friendship, talking, laughing, and crying. But not all of them are just about girlfriends. You see family, physical activities, hobbies, and time in nature. What a diverse list. There are some trends, of course: food and wine!

Hiking, walks, sit by the fire and sing

Sex, eating healthy, drinking wine, exercise, shopping, joking, dark humor, venting, day spa, massage, vacation, beach, long drive, sleeping children

Music, play, sleep, horseback riding, movies, taking breaks, socializing, hanging out with family, eating breakfast, eating dessert, reading, exercising, trips, beach, hiking

Humor, drinking wine, running, Target/coffee, music, bath/wine, crying, napping, driving, making lists

Drinking wine, listening to music, running, washing dishes, exercising, taking a bath, reading a book, snuggling w/kids, gardening, calling mom, going for drive, walking on beach

Eating chocolate, deep breathing, regular massage, gardening, reading, walking, sky gazing

Music
Cake
Glass of wine
Watch movies

Shop
Take a walk
Exercise
Snack
Working out
Drink
Sleep
Deep breathing
Time off
Exercise and wine!
Treadmill
Shop
Eat right
Food
Read a book

Laughter, working out, gardening, shopping, cooking, pets, eating, prayer, sharing feelings with friends, drinking wine, hunting, crying, reading

Swear jar, batting cages, exercise, sparring w/son, going out w/friends, laughing, walking, genuine smiling, listening to music

Music, swimming, working out, massage, pedicure, hugs, laughing, crying, quilting, happy hour w/friendship, shopping, traveling

Gambling, bathing in tub, reading, walking dog, brush it off

Walking, exercising, creating a plan, talking about anything other than what is stressing me out, perspective, being around fun people, Zumba, family time, shooting things

Girlfriends
Playing with kids
Chocolate
Manicure
Drink a glass of wine
Workout
Yoga

Taking walks
Shooting range
Wednesday night family dinner
Music
Walking
Cupcakes
Exercise
Eat
One hour of free time by myself
Quiet time/Sleep
Take a walk
Drink
Read

Listen, you don't need me or even fifty or a hundred other women telling you to take care of yourself. You already know that. At the end of every chapter up until here you've read advice from real women who have selflessly shared their lives with you. I hope seeing that has helped. And seeing more here from other *real* women should help, too. Add yours. Work on it by yourself, or work on it with a friend.

The moral of the story, the book, and the exit strategy is this:

We're not cats. We've been given only one life. It can and should be good. Don't let deodorant commercials lead you to believe it should not. Don't let Internet articles tell you it should not. Don't let other women tell you it should not. You are in charge of how your one life goes so:

- **Decide who you are**
- **Decide how you'll talk**
- **Decide how you'll take care of yourself**
- **Don't be lazy**
- **Rest**
- **Eat right**

- **Sleep**
- **Bond with women over other things—not stress**
- **Be a revolutionary in the war on stress!**
- **And . . . be happy!**

More life advice from real women–Elizabeth and Nancy:

Elizabeth: *I would tell her [a stressed-out friend] to sit down and evaluate specifically what it is about her life that's stressing her. At the moment, you may have to reevaluate multiple times, next week and maybe something different, next month, next year, but sit down and evaluate, kind of like the conversation we talked about. You know, what is it about your life that is stressing you? Is it the job? Is it relationship with hubby? Is it relationship with your kids or parents or whoever in your–the significant people in your life? Is it your children's schedules? . . . Identify what that is and then take steps to reduce that. Take steps, do what you have to, make some choices.*

Nancy: *If I had to sit down and tell anybody, and it's like, look, what's bothering you, and dump it. Why keep it if it's (**Elizabeth:** It's not that important.) . . . if it is that irritating, it's kind of like that festering pair of shoes. Throw the shoes away. If they hurt your feet, throw them away. (**Tami:** Don't keep wearing them.) Don't keep wearing the shoes.*

13
The Night Light

In the spring of '92, she had two bad experiences with teachers as she was doing her student teaching—very negative experiences where she was actually downgraded in front of students. She has attempted to put this out of her mind, but she is now ruminating and obsessed over these experiences. She feels panicked and scared. "My life is over. I feel like a failure." She states she wants the teaching job very badly but just can't get started. She is suffering major anxiety attacks with shortness of breath and heart palpitations. She feels very anxious about leaving her children, ages three, five, and seven. Husband is a police officer and is willing to help with the children in any way. He is very supportive.

FOR TEN YEARS I HAVE SHARED MY STORY OF ANXIETY. UNTIL I RETURNED to school to study stress, I always attributed my hospitalization to perfectionism. I would say something like this:

> *Growing up the way I did, all I wanted was to be perfect. To not be noticed. To make everyone happy and not make mistakes. So when two supervising teachers gave me negative feedback, I couldn't handle it. My perfectionism led me to believe I was a complete failure and that life would never be worth living again.*

I would read my medical records, mostly about my anger, feelings of worthlessness, and low self-esteem. And all those words were 100 percent true. Perfectionism was certainly a huge part of my path. But I would stop there, not realizing there was more—so much more to those medical records that I had been reading for years. Actually, the revelation comes from the words in the final three sentences of the opening passage above.

In the early years of healing, I knew nothing about the impact that identity had on my life. I never even considered societal expectations on women and the struggles we encounter. One day I was reading that story of leaving the children, and it slammed me like a ton of bricks:

Part of my anxiety was that I didn't know it was OK to be who I wanted to be.

Oh my gosh, how could I have missed that? How could I have not just said to my family, *Hey, I don't want to go to work full time right now—I want to be a mom!* Furthermore, how could *someone* have not picked up on my cry for help? It didn't matter that their father wanted to help. It wasn't true that *I wanted to teach very badly.* How in the world was that *not* abundantly clear? I mean, didn't these people go to school to sort of read between the lines? Or read between the screams?

I remember teaching a managing-emotions class in 2007. A young woman came up to me at the end of the day in tears; she was probably in her mid-twenties. She told me she had been married a few years, had her master's degree, and loved her job. She went on to describe a dinnertime conversation she had with her family. She mentioned that when she had children (she and her husband were trying to get pregnant), she wanted to stay home with them for a time. What happened next sent her into a tailspin of worry: this poor girl's family ambushed her with phrases like, *What? You're going to waste your education on staying home with* kids?! *You have a master's degree! You didn't do all that work to wipe noses, change diapers, and play with blocks!* And they continued to tear her down.

Oh, my. My heart ached for her, but I *still* didn't relate her experience to my own story. Looking back, I realize this young woman and I had both struggled with our own identity issues. And now, I think, *How dare society do this to us! How dare we let them!* But we can't stop it if we don't know it even exists or that we have choices. The Stress Club sucks! Yes, I said it—S.U.C.K.S. It has deep-rooted philosophical, religious, and cultural, hidden rules. Its wicked tentacles reach much further than the busyness we have during our days. They reach to our very core as women: who we think we are, who we say we are, and who we want to be. And we've been ill-equipped to disconnect from it. Until now.

So how did I finally come to a place where I was ready to get out? To cancel my lifetime membership?

In the introduction I mentioned that my husband checked my medical records and asked me what made me decide to change. I decided to save some of those details to close us out.

You know how sometimes you have to get up in the middle of the night and go to the bathroom? (For those of you who are about my age [fiftyish], you'll really identify.) Do you also try to keep your eyes as squinty as you can so you don't risk fully waking up? For a few years my husband and I would often pass each other in the night—back and forth. Sometimes we'd bump into each other. Sometimes I would run into the door. Occasionally, I'd hear him jam his toe on the bed. But then, this one particular night came! This is a little personal, but it makes a great point:

I'm in the bathroom, you know, sitting. I had my eyes closed as tightly as I could without being completely blind when, suddenly . . . I sensed a presence! My eyelids popped wide open to see my husband standing in front of me with his eyes pressed closed—in position, if you know what I mean! I screamed. He screamed. Phew. It was a close call.

The next day as we laughed about it, we talked about the amount of time and the kind of pain it took before we decided to make a change—at least to get a night light. This wasn't the first time our nighttime trips had caused problems. And even though we both walked around with squinty eyes, a nightlight would still have helped! I bought one that day.

Shortly after (summer of 2015), I was planning a new seminar called *# (Hashtag) The Challenge of Change,* and I decided this would be a great story to tell. I was talking to Tim about this, and in the midst of our conversation, I showed him my medical records. Now, he doesn't know the *old me*—the me who would lash out in anger. The me who threw things against the wall. The me who was described as *depressed, fearful, angry, frightened, helpless, hopeless, worthless, detached, and wished to be dead.* Here it is again—that powerful question:

So what made you decide to change?

Did I *decide*? Oftentimes I think, I didn't *decide* the experiences I had as a child, I didn't *decide* how they affected me, so how in the world could I *decide* to change? But he was right. *I* was the one who had to decide enough was enough.

As I'm writing today I realize it's been exactly twenty-one years since my hospitalization. The world was dark that day. Stagnant. Sad. Hopeless. So much has changed in twenty-one years. Today the world is bright. Ever-changing. Full of joy and hope. Still full of responsibilities and challenges. The bottom line is, I was *tired* of the old life. *Sooooo tired.* I didn't want to be angry or anxious or depressed or any of those other words anymore.

The years that followed my release from the hospital weren't exactly sunshine, lollipops, and rainbows. For several years after, I lived on Zoloft (an antidepressant) and Klonopin (a minor tranquilizer). I recall one day in particular. It was a school/work day for us all. I was getting ready when a massive panic attack struck, and I told my husband I couldn't do it anymore. I got in the car and drove off. Looking back, I can't imagine how he must have felt. Thankfully, I had taken a Klonopin before I left, so after a bit of time passed I came down from the attack. I drove home, finished getting ready, and went about my day. Now, I was only half a person on those medicated days, but I got through it. If you're reading this and you're on antidepressants or tranquilizers, please know that I'm pro medication. My only complaint is the way these medications are managed. Never feel like you've given up or you have no faith if medication is what you need. Just be sure that you are part of the decision and that you take other steps to heal your mind.

Days, weeks, and months passed and I progressed. Several years later my marriage ended, and I found myself living the life of a single mom. It was difficult for sure, but so many great things happened during those years. I bought a house all by myself and finished my master's degree. I rediscovered my relationship with God and grew closer to my children. We lived in a great family neighborhood, so we always had friends around. *And* I found out I was strong, capable, and independent!

The *biggest* event of those years was meeting my husband, Tim. I first laid eyes on him in November 2001 in my singles' Sunday school class, and couldn't help but notice he was adorable. I was selling tickets for our New Year's Eve dance and asked him if he'd like to buy one. He responded, *Oh, I'm sorry, I was raised very strict Pentecostal. I don't dance.* Yikes! He didn't laugh. Didn't say, *Just kidding.* Didn't do *anything* that indicated he was kidding. For several weeks after that, he would come to class right on time and leave immediately after. He didn't stay to socialize, go to lunch, or even chat.

Eventually we wound up sitting at the same table, and he began to open up. He told us he had five kids. *Five kids! Wow!* But there was more: only one of them was his. He had been married before as well, and he and his wife planned their life carefully: One child. God has such a sense of humor, Tim always says. Shortly after his only child turned sixteen (I didn't know him then, by the way), he was in his office in Nashville, Tennessee. The phone rang, and it was a social worker from Colorado: *We have four of your sister's six children here with us* (two of them were already grown). *Your sister has had some problems over the years. Would you like to adopt them?* He didn't even know his sister had six kids—she had been out of his life for many years.

Talk about life changing fast! He and his wife went from one to five children in a matter of months. Then their marriage ended. Then he met me and my three children, and the rest, as they say, is history!

We married in 2003 and blended this crazy family together. It was hard but fun. Supportive but demanding. Spattered with conflict but also overflowing with love. Tim had to learn how to raise girls. I had to learn how to treat a husband. He had to let me act in ways moms do, and I had to allow him to act in ways dads do. We had to figure out how to handle money and household duties. And pets! Oh my goodness, pets.

I didn't know right away, but this man would become my rock, my supporter, my cheerleader, my encourager, and my best friend. He is the one who urged me to return to school to study this stress thing and then put up with me when it got tough. And we really were against the odds: Eight children combined, both of us divorced, financial issues at one point, my travel. So much. But our unique life together has grown us both in so many ways.

We have had so many changes over the years. In 2005 I left ten years of teaching to write my first book, *Life Without the Monsters*, and start speaking to groups. Then I started traveling, leaving this poor man alone with five children in middle and high school! At one point, we lost almost everything we owned when his business partner was implicated in a Ponzi scheme. We had children graduate, go to college, get married, and move away. We had new sons and daughters-in-law and then grandchildren. He changed jobs. My career ebbed and flowed. So, so much. And yet, we remained best friends and partners. Today, our children are all grown up and spread out a bit. Tim and I are still living the dream in southern California and loving it.

Here's an update on the parent situation. As of the printing of this book, my father still has his health problems but is doing pretty well. My mother? It's been a rough go, and her story is one that can give any woman hope (in a weird sort of way).

For forty years I have been praying for my mother. Praying for her bitterness to fade. Praying for peace and love in her life. I prayed that she would forgive my father and start living her own life, without the crippling guilt she dumped on my sister and me. The bitterness and refusal to take care of herself led to one health problem after another, both physical and mental. I prayed for that.

I'll be honest: for many years I kept a safe emotional distance from her. Being around the manipulation, anger, depression, and guilt pulled me down, and I couldn't allow myself to sink to those places anymore. But my sister fared far worse than I did since Mom had lived with her most of her life. So the emotional scars my sister has are many and deep.

In 2013 we finally moved our mother out of my sister's house into a senior apartment complex. I can't even begin to describe what her bedroom looked like as we cleaned it out. Suffice it to say we had to throw away the mattress and box springs, and replace the carpet. That brought back some serious childhood nightmares.

Since her new place wasn't assisted living or a nursing home, we paid a home health agency to manage her medications and monitor her health. Well, let me tell you . . . she *hated* that we *put* her there! She was filled with more anger and bitterness, and she refused to participate in life there. She wouldn't go to the dining room, so her aides started bringing meals to her room. She stopped getting dressed, taking showers, or washing her hair. It got so bad that she wouldn't even get up to go to the bathroom. All of this affected her physical health, and within months she was on 24/7 oxygen and in a wheelchair. Mentally? well, at one point a psychiatrist actually said this: *She has "can't get her shit together" syndrome.* We were actually hoping there was some undiscovered illness that might explain her behavior and allow a newfound course of treatment. No. Years of depression was all.

In 2015, we finally decided it was time for assisted living; she needed more help than we could give her on our own. Living with my sister wasn't an option anymore, and I traveled for a living. What has happened over the last two years has been nothing short of a miracle! In the beginning, she once again wanted to retreat from life, but staff where she lived refused to let her sit in her room. They made her come to the dining room for lunch and dinner. They came to her room and escorted her to bingo. They went out to lunch once or twice a month as a group, and she always went. They let her leave her apartment door open so she could feel a part of the activity up and down the hallways. In this environment full of hustle and bustle, she blossomed! No more wheelchair. No more 24/7 oxygen. Every day a new outfit and makeup. She was a rock star!

But something else happened at the same time: she developed dementia. Now, you might be prepared for a sad story, but that's not what you're going to read. After forty years of praying, God healed my mother through dementia. During the past two years, she had forgotten she was angry. She was unable to feel bitterness anymore. She couldn't remember how to be manipulative. She was the sweetest, happiest, most easygoing woman you would ever want to meet. She was the favorite patient everywhere she went. A miracle!

But as this book goes to print, things changed again. On October 10, 2016, my mom left us. It was actually a much shorter journey than I had anticipated. On October 3 we placed her in hospice care. All those health problems took their toll, and the doctors couldn't make her better anymore. Mom has always been more like a child than an adult, and the dementia took that to a whole new level. We tried talking with her about how much fight she had in her, but that only led to her feeling terrified that she might be at the end of her life. So we moved forward telling her it was all going to be OK. And it really is. We didn't know if she'd be with us for another day or for another six months, but it was time to stop putting her through crazy treatments that were never going to cure her. It was time to let her eat bologna and ice cream for dinner if she wanted. No more CT scans, radiation treatments, steroids, and bronchoscopies. They loved her at her assisted living apartment, and she loved them. So my sister and I joined with them and the sweet hospice people and let her be, as we now say, *happily demented.*

Her biggest fear was dying alone, and that did not happen. My sister and I were there. One of her dearest friends was there. Many of the women who took care of her were there. We held her hand and stroked her hair. We told her we loved her. We told her it was OK to go, that we'd be OK. I'm not going to lie—the dying part was horrific, not peaceful at all. I'm still processing those emotions, but the nurses assured me she felt no pain. And that gives me peace.

How can this possibly inspire? First, there is always hope. I sometimes hear the phrase, *She'll (or he'll) never change!* I hate that phrase. We don't know what life holds for us or for anyone else. Each of us has our own path, and some women's paths are more painful than others. But change comes in many forms. For my mother, it came with dementia. And what a total blessing! A woman who was angry, bitter, manipulative, and fearful of everything was now sweet, happy, and honestly a joy to be around. Those who knew her loved her. The dementia kept her from living the last few years of her life with paralyzing fear. Instead, she lived each day thinking she would be better. Second, no one ever taught my mother how to deal with the daily situations in life. How to be her own person. How to live her own identity outside of being a mother and a wife. How to forgive. We can be women who not only learn these concepts, but also teach them to younger women in our lives. We can be wise, courageous leaders of a revolution of our minds!

I hope our stories—from the various women you've met in this book as well as mine—have provided some insights into the Stress Club and provided you with the motivation and direction to get out. The power is in you. Although my study focused on a small level, the conversation itself, it is clear there are broader implications. Our conversations are embedded in webs of complex sociological practices. Within our families, for example, there are expectations placed upon us that influence how we talk. I don't mean to be a downer here, but today we women are still expected to do the majority of childcare and housework, to be good mothers and daughters, and to perform as superwomen. At work, we are expected to speak up, but not too much. We're allowed to have identities as career women, but we'd better make it work for the family. And as some workplaces support a culture of stress, the risks are great if we're not in the club. Right?

As Betty Friedan noted in 1963, the world of advertising holds considerable power over us. In Friedan's era, it was blenders and toasters that would make women happy. Today's advertisers' connections to the Stress Club are yet to be studied, but they are there. Examples include mattresses that help women living in *the real world* sleep better; an herbal supplement that will help us be more alert and organized when we're stressed; deodorant that will minimize *stress sweat;* and makeup that will make us look like we've had eight hours of sleep, even if we haven't. The influence advertisers have over our identities is powerful. And since we control about 70 percent of global consumer spending, little motivation exists for advertisers to change this conversation, since that would translate into a drop in sales for stress-related products. So it's up to us to take our power back. A revolution!

During the time I was being admitted to the hospital, I wasn't sure life would ever be worth living again. I had lived a life dictated by what others thought of me and expected of me. The stress of simple, everyday life had become unbearable. The conversations in this book contain women's stories. They shared stories of working long hours. They described their burdens and responsibilities. They spoke of the need for more me time to exercise and relax. What I struggled to relay to you were their deeper stories, their tears, their pain and feelings of helplessness to make their lives better. This is the true reason for this study. My hope is that you will become more aware of the path you are taking and truly seek the life you so deeply desire.

Are you ready for your personal revolution? Are you ready to stop participating in the Stress Club, take your power back, and start living your own life? I will end our time together with a modified version of my husband's powerful question— a question I hope will fuel your life from this day forward:

What will make you decide to change?

Final life advice from real women—Lydia and Dalia:

Lydia: *Talk to a friend? I talk to Dalia and she'll talk to me. So, things that we might not tell anyone else, and it helps just to have that.*

Dalia: *To not feel alone in it. Just to not feel alone in it. I felt comforted coming here, because I don't have to see Lydia every day, but I know she's here. But when I know she's not here? I'm concerned and I want to know why she's not here. I want to know what she needs. . . . You can't always find that person that you connect with, so I wouldn't necessarily say talk, but find something or someone, an activity or someone, that even if you're talking about what your stresses are, that you get a peace at the same time with it.*

I wish you comfort, connection, and peace.

Notes

1. American Psychological Association, *Stress in America: Our Health at Risk*. Washington, DC: Anderson, B., et al., 2012, p. 5.
2. Rosch, P. (1984). "The Effects of Stress on Women," *The Female Patient* 9, 14–32. Retrieved January 20, 2001, from www.stress.org/archives/FP.pdf.
3. Friedan, Betty, T*he Feminine Mystique.* New York: W.W. Norton, 1963, p. 61.
4. McKenna, E., *When Work Doesn't Work Anymore: Women, Work, and Identity*. New York, New York: Delacorte Press, 1997, p. 11.
5. Bennetts, L., T*he Feminine Mistake: Are We Giving Up Too Much?* New York: Voice/Hyperion, 2007, p. xxv.
6. Wetherell, M. (2011). *The Discursive Psychological Perspective.* [Video file] Retrieved from http://www.youtube.com/watch?v=H6IhIa2SRd4.
7. Coates, J. *Women Talk*. Cambridge, Massachusetts: Rockwell Publishers, 1996, p. 240.
8. Holmes TH, Raphe RH (1967). "The Social Readjustment Rating Scale." J Psychoses Res. 11 (2): 213–8. doi:10.1016/0022-3999(67)90010-4.
9. Lazarus, R., *Psychological Stress and the Coping Process.* New York: McGraw-Hill, 1996, p. 17.
10. Kranz, K., & Long, B. (2002). "Messages about Stress in Two North American Women's Magazines: Helpful? We Think Not!" *Feminism and Psychology*, 12, 525-530. Retrieved August 28, 2011, from http://fap.sagepub.com/content/12/4/525.)

11. Ibid.
12. West, Tami, *Life Without the Monsters*, 2006, pp. 78-79.
13. *Time Magazine,* October 26, 2009, p. 29.
14. Miller, J. B., *Toward a New Psychology of Women.* Boston: Beacon Press, 1976, pp. xii-xiii.
15. Josselson, R., *Finding Herself: Pathways to Identity Development in Women.* San Francisco: Jossey-Bass, 1987, p. 183.
16. *Time Magazine*, October 26, 2009, p. 29.

Additional Resource:

Tannen, Deborah, *You Just Don't Understand: Women and Men in Conversation* (audiobook), Recorded Books, 2008.

About the Author

Dr. TAMI WEST HAS BEEN HELPING WOMEN TAKE THEIR POWER BACK and live their own lives for more than fifteen years. Her passion stems from a lifelong battle with anxiety disorder, which inspired her to devote her career to helping women with their emotional health.

Her clients come from all walks of life. Danbury Federal Prison inmates (the setting of the Netflix Emmy-winning series *Orange is the New Black*, as well as the prison home for Martha Stewart and Real Housewife Teresa Garduci) found Tami to be genuine and real, with good practical messages and coping skills. Social Security Administration senior management called her "a true professional and fantastic at what she does!"

After earning a bachelor's degree in biology, Tami spent the next ten years working in hospitals, physician's offices, and research labs. She changed careers in 1995, becoming a public school teacher, and in 2005 decided to pursue a career that would allow her to use personal experiences to help women find solutions to their challenges.

Tami's undergraduate degrees in science and education, as well as her doctoral research and degree in human development, uniquely equip her to address the human factors that help determine the success of women, both personally and professionally.

She has spoken to groups in forty-eight states across the United States, the United Kingdom, Australia, and New Zealand. When she's not speaking or writing, you might find her with her husband at the beach, reading historical fiction, at Disneyland, or watching *Big Bang Theory*.

Made in the USA
Columbia, SC
13 September 2021

44781214R00138